SPIRITUAL INFUSION

Twelve-Step Recovery and Revival
Inside and Outside the Church

Patt Manna

Spiritual INFUSION

Twelve-Step Recovery and Revival Inside and Outside the Church

VMI Publishers • Sisters, Oregon

The excerpts from the book of Alcoholics Anonymous are reprinted with permission of Alcoholics Anonymous World Services, Inc. (A.A.WS). Permission to reprint these excerpts does not mean that A.A.WS has reviewed or approved the contents of this publication, or that A.A.WS necessarily agrees with the views expressed herein. A.A. is a program of recovery from alcoholism only. Use of these excerpts in connection with programs and activities that are patterned after A.A. but that address other problems does not imply otherwise.

Scripture verses marked NIV are taken from the *Holy Bible, New International Version*. Copyright © 1973, 19780 1984 by International Bible Society. Used by permission of Zondervan Publishing House. All rights reserved.

Scripture marked NKJV are taken from the *New King James Version*. Copyright © 1982 by Thomas Nelson, Inc. Used by permission. All rights reserved.

Scripture quotations marked KJV are taken from the *21ˢᵗ Century King James Version*. Copyright © 1994. Used by permission of Deuel Enterprises, Inc., Gary, SD 57237. All rights reserved.

Scripture quotations marked NLT are taken from the *Holy Bible, New Living Translation*. Copyright © 1996, 2004. Used by permission of Tyndale House Publishers, Inc., Wheaton, Illinois 60189. All rights reserved.

Published by
VMI Publishers
Sisters, Oregon
www. vmipublishers.com

ISBN 13: 9781935265085
ISBN 10: 1935265083

Library of Congress: 2009930079

Printed in the USA

Cover design by Juanita Dix, j.d. Design, www.designjd.net

DEDICATION

This book is dedicated with love to all my children and my children's children as well as my wonderful husband for encouraging me to carry this message.

TABLE OF CONTENTS

Introduction 9

Chapter 1: Study of "How It Works" 13

Chapter 2: Study of "The How & Why of It" 59

Chapter 3: Study of "The Promises" 65

Chapter 4: Study of "Acceptance" 73

Chapter 5: Study of "A Vision for You" 75

Chapter 6: Study of "Serenity Prayer" 79

Chapter 7: Testimonies 87

Suggested Reading 119

Selected Bibliography 123

INTRODUCTION

You need to understand what the word "antecedent" means when dealing with addicted people. The synonyms for "antecedent" are "precursor," "forerunner," "predecessor," and "forebear." So to understand what "antecedent" means is to accept the fact that something has to exist before something else can happen. Alcohol, drugs, pornography, or gambling use is the antecedent of addiction, and *addiction* is the antecedent of crime.

One consistent variable within the onset of criminality is the existing antecedent of alcohol/drug/pornography/gambling use, abuse, and addiction. Society at large can only build so many prisons and jails to house a symptom of the real problem. Crime is a symptom! Alcohol/drug/pornography/gambling *use* is the antecedent of addiction, and *addiction* is the antecedent of crime. The key to transformation from addiction is available to all.

It is important to make a clear distinction between use (make use of, avail yourself of) and abuse (misuse). The term "addict" should only be used if the individual is abusing and dependent on alcohol or drugs or pornography or gambling. It should be noted that it is impossible to become an addict unless one is first a user. Therefore, use is the first step toward addiction. Addiction is a separate and even more self-defeating force that abuses a person's freedom and makes them do things they really do not want to do.

Addictions are never single problems. Each of our major addictions consists of multiple others that have been affected by it. Breaking an addiction requires changes in many areas of our lives. The struggle of trying to stop smoking will be greater, for example, after eating, or at other times that have become associated with cigarettes. An alcoholic is likely to slip if he or she frequents their old drinking well just to play darts. A narcotic addict will relapse if he or she continues to associate with the same old friends. A gambler will relapse if he or she eats in a casino just because the food is good. The overeater won't get better by obsessing over food commercials on television.

Regardless of how an addiction begins, the longer it stays out of control the more powerful it becomes. Stress and chaos build another addiction around our major addictions to protect the death grip it has, like a spreading disease steadily invading and encompassing our surroundings, including our families.

It is here that I want to give you an invitation to transformation. I have written for you my personal commentary and study of the recovery tool of *How It Works* and more. Before each Twelve Step meeting, a particular portion of chapter five out of The Big Book, called *How It Works*, is read by one of the members of the group as everyone else listens and savors every word. I personally would soak in this process of *How It Works* as I tried to grasp *It*. Several months went by before I could remember any part of *It* to quote *It*. I only remembered how good I felt when hearing *How It Works* read. More months passed before I could quote the steps as well, but I loved every minute while listening to them being read. Nevertheless, I knew that what I read and heard was going to restore what my addiction had taken from me, and I would find my purpose in life.

I am a believer in *How It Works* who has struggled with alcohol, prescription drugs, and codependent behaviors. The first time I was introduced to the Twelve Step Program of Alcoholics Anonymous (A.A.), it gave me sobriety (abstinence, clear-headedness) from alcohol. Before I began the fourth step of the program I balked from the pain that was oozing out of me. My sponsor sent me to Adult Children of Alcoholics (ACA) and Codependents Anonymous (CoDa) to find myself and identify where this pain was coming from. There was a definition of depression that was repeated around the recovery rooms, and it was not pleasant. The definition goes like this: Depression is like self-pity oozing from every pore. In other words, my sponsor recognized her limitations, and I recognized her frustration in working with me. The last thing my sponsor told me was to attend my chemically dependent meeting daily. So, I went to three or four or more meetings every day. First I went to meetings for my primary addiction of alcohol, then I started to attend other Twelve Step Programs. I am still grateful to this day for what I learned about myself in all Twelve Step Fellowships, because it was the same method and course of action in the process of peeling this onion one layer at a time. Another big lesson I learned right away was that it was not my sponsor's responsibility to fix me, but my responsibility to make my recovery happen through God's mercy and grace. So, the sooner I stopped feeling sorry for myself and got into action, the sooner I would get to the promises that this Twelve Step Program claimed were mine to have.

I am an old-timer in this Twelve Step Program, and I desperately want to have a personal meeting with you to share my experience, strength, and hope through *How It Works*. Come join me now as we drink from the existing well of the Twelve Step recovery revival on our journey to another level of recovery and release the revival in you. You will read study excerpts quoted from the original text and proceed to study it with me line upon line, precept upon precept, directly following the quoted text.

Chapter One

Study of

"How It Works"

Here is a simple study approach to use. I learned it when attending an Inductive Bible Study course. It involves three basic skills: observation, interpretation, and application.

1) Observation answers the question: What does the text say?
2) Interpretation answers the question: What does the text mean?
3) Application answers the question: What does the text mean to me personally? What truths can I put into practice? What changes should I make in my life?

When you know what the text says, what the text means, and how to put the text's truths into practice, you will be equipped for every circumstance of life. These tools helped me transform my life and gain a deep and abiding relationship with a power greater than myself, and I know they will help you to do the same.

This begins the study of Chapter 5, "How It Works," starting on pages 58–60 of the Third Edition of Alcoholics Anonymous' Big Book.

STUDY EXCERPT: "RARELY HAVE we seen a person fail who has thoroughly followed our path."

Look closely at the first two words of the sentence. Both are capitalized. This is consistent for the beginning paragraphs throughout the chapters of this book. More than one word is capitalized. Why is this? I believe the authors wanted to drive the point home on the deeper meaning of those particular words. When writing an email, if you capitalize in your message, you are considered to be yelling. That is what I believe we need to consider here when reading this text.

The synonyms for "rarely" are "hardly ever," "not often," "on the odd occasion," "infrequently," or "seldom." The word "have" is uniquely used, because it is the present perfect tense. So when you read this it means the same today as it did yesterday, and it will mean the same tomorrow as it did today. Then "rarely have" surely intensifies and confirms the need to be seen in meetings. So, go to meetings, keep coming back and you will not fail!

This program is about life (recovery) or death (failure). Every day I put my feet on the floor, get up, and participate in being alive I will have to make choices. When I come to a fork in the road I will have to choose between life and death. "I call heaven and earth as witnesses today against you, that I have set before you life and death, blessing and cursing; therefore choose life, that both you and your descendants may live" (Deuteronomy 30:19, NKJV). Choose life!

In the book *The Road Less Traveled* by M. Scott Peck, I found an understanding of the meaning of love that I could accept at an early time in my recovery on the path to life. M. Scott Peck simply revealed that love was the willingness to nurture my own and another human being's spiritual growth. Wow! So, I accepted this program as life and death for me, and no matter what I felt about other people in this program I could love them as people on a journey with a common malady. I had begun my spiritual quest.

In M. Scott Peck's book *People of the Lie*, I found an understanding of evil that I could also accept at that same early time in my recovery. The word "evil" means anything destructive to another human being's spiritual growth. To do evil is to be on the path to death. I have recognized people who are under the influence of evil, for they promote confusion rather than the facts or truth.

Now properly armed with facts (truth) about love and evil, I stepped onto the path of that road less traveled. Until this new understanding was reached, I feared that I could not be of use to another human being on this journey, let alone my family and myself. The words "thoroughly followed our path" convinced me that one of the most important things to do in preparing for a journey was to find the best roads leading to the ultimate destination. This was thoroughly following the roads suggested by others (old-timers), who stepped onto that path less taken and trudged this road to happy destiny. If we are not sure of our road or direction, we take the chance of driving on an uncharted highway and may ultimately be in the same predicament over and over again, only to remain lost. Many people remain lost in the program, because they are attempting to follow the wrong directions. They do not study the basic text! They work the program to their own destruction, not because they are not active in the program, but because they have acquired, willingly, the wrong viewpoint towards recovery. These people are known as retreads, relapsers, slippers, backsliders. They are working the program with the wrong attitudes and intentions, which will ultimately lead to death. Check your motives. Choose life!

I have seen with my own eyes the man-made hell on earth that people live because of the "in and out of the program" programs. You meet them at various meetings, then they are gone to treatment, then they are back, then they are gone to jail, then they are back, then they are gone to prison, then they are back, then they are gone. You do not have to go back out of the program. I give you permission to stay! Continuous sobriety is possible. Choose life!

In the original manuscript of The Big Book, the word "direction" was the word originally suggested instead of the word "path" that was finally chosen. What a revelation that was! The word "direction" is synonymous with orders and commands. Those who wrote the book knew that addicted people do not want to be told, ordered, or commanded to do anything. So it definitely leaves the words "followed our path" to be the way out of addiction as suggested only.

STUDY EXCERPT: "Those who do not recover are people who cannot or will not completely give themselves to this simple program, usually men and women who are constitutionally incapable of being honest with themselves. There are such unfortunates. They are not at fault; they seem to have been born that way. They are naturally incapable of grasping and developing a manner of living which demands rigorous honesty. Their chances are less than average."

The simple program is exactly what it is: simple. The steps are in order from one through twelve. Each step, if properly worked, has its own level of humility that must be experienced before proceeding to the next step. You cannot buy humility, nor can you read about humility and think that you will become a humble person.

Humility must be experienced. For example, I was on my way home from my second or third meeting, I had not said a word or uttered a sound except to cry continuously. I knew the moment would come soon when I would have to say, "My name is Patt, and I am an alcoholic." I said it every which way but loose and choked on it every time as I practiced identifying with those words. Then I looked in the mirror after I got home and said it again without hesitation and wept desperately for a new life. Then one evening, a woman started to share in the meeting. After she introduced herself, she immediately said, "I'm an alcoholic, and I had become a liar, a cheat, and a thief." Her words haunted me for days. Everyone dreads the moment when we suddenly see ourselves for what we have become. That is to stand face to face with the truth of ourselves as selfish, deceitful, and full of excuses, dishonesty to ourselves, and faults. So keep it simple, do it one step at a time, and gradually you can motivate your daily living with the truth instead of the habits, the hurts, and the hang-ups of addictions.

It has been said that honesty, willingness, and open mindedness are the essentials for recovery in all Twelve Step programs. Old-timers will tell you that the core of this program is to get honest with yourself, clean house, and help others. Many of us have a history of being liars, of continually lying both to ourselves and others. In the Bible there are many stories about the transformations of liars, cheats, thieves, and murderers. For example, Jacob was a lying, double-dealing man, and when he found that power greater than himself, he became Israel. When Saul found this power greater than himself, he became Paul on the road to Damascus.

Johnny Cash (the man in black) wrote a book titled *The Man in White* and produced an evangelistic documentary of *The Gospel Road*. Yes, Johnny Cash found this power greater than himself. Billy Graham had a blurb on the hardcover jacket of *The Man in White* that mentioned how Johnny Cash had written the most in-depth portrayal of the transformation that took place on the Damascus Road. Billy Graham also mentioned in that blurb that he used Johnny Cash's documentary as an evangelistic tool.

This means that anyone can change once they find that power greater than themselves. For without rigorous honesty, the program would be nothing more nor less than a continuation of a life full of conning and hypocrisy. Transformation must take place through surrender and repentance. Surrender alone will not take you there, as this is a matter of the heart and you must go deeper. So there must be conviction. It must be honesty day in and day out, hour in and hour out, minute in and minute out, or there is less chance for recovery.

My personal cry was, "God help me, what a mess I have made of my life!" For some who can't get honest, it may take a divine appointment and it is God's grace alone that can pierce their hardened shell. His grace was able to pierce my hardened shell and flow into my emptiness where something new was able to grow. The understanding of this fresh information about a recovery process took root for me immediately, and the revelations that surfaced were clearer, simpler, and more beautiful than I ever could have asked for. There was no turning back for me.

Months later, my sponsor made me start using a dictionary and start looking up words of which I really did not have a clear understanding. For example, the first word I had to look up was "rigorous." As I fumbled through the dictionary, I found that the synonyms for "rigorous" are "exact," "meticulous," "painstaking," "accurate," "scrupulous," "laborious," "rough," "harsh," and "severe." For somebody like me who thought she knew it all, this was a learning experience. So, you should have noticed by now that I have added the synonyms for many words in this study to try to get you to the deeper meaning and expand your thinking.

STUDY EXCERPT: "There are those, too, who suffer from grave emotional and mental disorders, but many of them do recover if they have the capacity to be honest."

One of the biggest obstacles to recovering from addiction is the denial that there is a problem. Take the words "grave" and "disorders." The synonyms for "grave" are "severe," "critical," and "serious." The synonyms for "disorder" are "confusion," "turmoil," "unrest," and "chaos." Many of us have had to fight our way through a lifetime of grave disorders without the capacity to be honest with ourselves or others. We can only use being in denial as a defense until we receive and process the knowledge about the truth of the problem concerning our addiction. Then denial can no longer be used as a defense, and it becomes rebellion against the truth. Without God's Word, which is the truth, life makes no sense.

There were occasions when I did have a glimpse of my problem but dismissed it immediately. The first glimpse was when all management personnel where I worked had to sit in on a presentation called Chalk Talk. The person giving the lecture happened to be a priest by the name of Father Martin. For just a split second I felt like he was talking to me, but then everyone was laughing and smirking about the big drunks in our office, so I dismissed it and said no problem because I was nothing like them. Another time, I had called my mother to chat (or, in other words, to cry and feel sorry for myself) and she questioned me and asked if I was drinking. I was, but I lied and said, "No." Immediately, I gave an excuse and got off the phone with her. There in my confusion I questioned how she knew I was drinking. Suddenly I realized it was because she heard the ice clink in my glass when I took a drink in between words. So, I never used ice in my drinks again. No problem!

Depth Psychology and Compulsion—Alcoholism and Moral Responsibility, authored by John C. Ford in 1951, expressed that addicted people who have longevity of sobriety have achieved it and maintained it because someone, somewhere, rebuilt their human confidence, and as a result led them to a confidence and faith in the Divine, which ultimately is the only real security we have.

Gerald G. May, M. D., author of *Addiction & Grace*, contributed to the world of recovery by expressing that love and spirituality go hand in hand in the healing of addictions. He wrote that getting out of the bondage of addiction and into God's grace happens only through honesty.

I had not thought about recovery as a three-fold recovery of spiritual (spirit), mental (soul), and physical (body) healing. We think primarily of the physical realm when we long to be in God's grace and out of the bondage of addiction. So now we leave Egypt, which symbolizes bondage, for the Promised Land, which reflects freedom. We must claim our spiritual longing. Our hope is to be freed from having to cling to anything as a substitute for God. This is our spiritual freedom. I was forty years old when I left Egypt. I may not have arrived at The Promised Land yet, but at least I have left my Egypt. This is a spiritual journey for the rest of my life. We are all after the same happiness and peace of mind, which is called emotional sobriety. This is our mental freedom. Take this step of faith now, and make your own exodus with the rest of us; get out of your Egypt!

STUDY EXCERPT: "Our stories disclose in a general way what we used to be like, what happened, and what we are like now."

Building trust through repeated risks of faith is no different from many other processes of learning. We repeat a behavior, find it to be good and trustworthy, and the cells of our brains become more accepting of it in the future. Then as our trust grows, it becomes easier to take the next risk. The measure of faith is the degree to which we are really willing to risk telling the truth about what we used to be like, what happened to us, and what we are like now.

When I listened to the old-timers (members with five to forty years of sobriety when I came in the program) like Ernie K., Cliff B., Barney Z., Dee S., Nurse Judy, Furniture Judy, Birtie, and Clyde tell their testimonies, I received hope that there was another way to live. They were always in the meetings and were committed to service work.

I remember asking myself that one morning, while calling Alcoholics

Anonymous for help, "Is this it? Is this how it is going to be the rest of my life?" My addiction story ended with this scenario: I drank, I blacked out, and then I drank until I passed out. I came to in the morning to find a full drink on my nightstand. I took the drink to the kitchen, poured it down the sink, and shamed myself. Then I went through the kitchen looking for the bottle to see how much I had drunk. At the end of the scenario, I came to in the morning to find a full drink on my nightstand. I began to put the full drink in the refrigerator for a later experience rather than pouring it out. Then I went through the kitchen looking for the bottle to see how much I had left to start with the next day. Somehow deep inside I hoped it could be different. As I listened to the two women who came to my home at approximately 4:30 A.M., I knew I was going to be okay. They told me their stories of experience, strength, and hope. They told me I was sick and I was going to get well. But most of all, they told me about a God who loved me. Oh, how I needed to hear that God really loved me.

It was about 6:30 A.M. when my daughter came into the living room to see what was going on. One of the ladies asked my daughter if she wanted to see her mother get sober. She answered, "Yes!" My daughter could not imagine how my getting sober was going to affect her future. As the ladies were leaving they told me they would be back to pick me up at 11:00 A.M. to attend my first Twelve Step meeting. Those two women took me to my first meeting at a mental hospital/treatment facility. The meeting began with the normal readings of *How It Works* and the Twelve Steps. Then the patients, who were dressed in pajamas and robes without belts, shared their experience, strength, and hope. All of what they shared made so much sense to me. These patients were honest and so willing to tell me that I was in the right place, doing the right thing. The comedy of it all was that they were in a mental ward telling me I was going to be okay, and I believed them! I knew I was hearing the truth, and they gave me hope.

STUDY EXCERPT: "If you have decided you want what we have and are willing to go to any length to get it, then you are ready to take certain steps."

After my first meeting in the mental hospital, I was fully persuaded that wherever I was going had to be better than where I had been. I was willing to be willing. There was something so profound to me about attending my first meeting on a mental ward. I thought about it for hours, then called my little brother, who is six years younger than me. I told him I was in the Twelve Step Program. He was so excited for me. My brother said, "Patt, I didn't know what else to say to you." You see, my little brother had been clean and sober for ten years by way of the Twelve Steps before I got to the program. I honestly did not know that it was the Twelve Steps that had changed him so completely. He was always kind to me even if I did call him while I was drunk. Sometimes he would just stop by and see me and talk about calm things. I don't even remember what we talked about, because I was usually drinking and centered on myself. I just knew he always made me feel good. There was no condemnation from him.

But what I do remember was that my little brother had been committed to Western State Hospital for the Criminally Insane for three years as a direct result of drugs and alcohol. My brother spent his twenty-first birthday in that ward. Every Thursday night there was a Twelve Step meeting, and a little old lady from the program would pat him on the head and tell him that God saved him for something very special. He was sober for ten years before I made it to recovery. I believe my little brother planted a seed in my head about where to go when I was done with my insanity. Now I reflect back on why I looked in the yellow pages under alcohol and made that call in my desperation.

So at every meeting I listened with enthusiasm to those who shared their stories. I wanted what they had. I began to feel an element of peace that I had not felt since I was a young child. When my compliance showed up, all I wanted was to be in meetings to hear more and do whatever was suggested in the program. I went to a minimum of three meetings per day during the week and five to six meetings a day on the weekends. I never once thought about not going to a meeting. I ran home from meetings to clean house, put in a load of wash, do whatever with the kids (if they were around), go to work, then go back to another meeting. For one hour at a time, I felt safe and the hunger driving me was being fed. I was no longer lonely. At the end of every meeting they would say in unison, "Keep coming back. *It* works, if you work *It*." So I kept coming back!

> STUDY EXCERPT: "At some of these we balked. We thought we could find an easier, softer way. But we could not. With all the earnestness at our command, we beg of you to be fearless and thorough from the very start. Some of us have tried to hold on to our old ideas and the result was nil until we let go absolutely."

The old-timers told me to read for myself. If I would study the basic text of the Twelve Step Program, then I would know for sure what the real truth was. "My people are destroyed for lack of knowledge" (Hosea 4:6, KJV). I didn't believe people who quoted that text in meetings until I read The Big Book and knew what the truth was for myself. My brother told me to be careful of the counterfeits. I tested people's words against the text of the program, just as it tells us in the Bible to test everything by the Word of God. These counterfeits are inside and outside of the Twelve Step Programs and inside and outside the church. You will know these people, for they promote confusion rather than the facts (truth).

Throughout my years spent in the rooms of recovery both inside and outside of the church, I have watched members confronted with the Twelve Step Program who did not want it. This program is a big order to handle. So many members with their habits and excuses for not taking the steps have never fully, honestly, or literally worked the Twelve Steps. Why is this? Many just want to escape responsibility, minimize guilt, and justify themselves in their old ways. You will know these people by the chaos and confusion that follow them. "Brothers, if someone is caught in a sin, you who are spiritual should restore him gently. But watch yourself, or you also may be tempted" (Galatians 6:1, NIV).

> STUDY EXCERPT: "Remember that we deal with alcohol—cunning, baffling, powerful! Without help it is too much for us. But there is One who has all power—that One is God. May you find Him now!"

One of the biggest issues I had in my recovery was religion. I believed in God, but I did not believe God. Think about that last sentence again. I did not have the Bible in my entire life. What I did hear in church didn't match up with the world I lived in. I didn't get it. I never got past the altar at church. But, I would soon find out about the reality of Jesus.

An old-timer named Barney Z gave me a book titled *The Sermon on the Mount*, by Emmet Fox. Barney told me that the co-founders of the Twelve Step Program used this book and the Bible in their beginning days. As I began to study the history of A.A., I found this to be true, with an emphasis on the Book of James, Matthew's Sermon on the Mount, and the thirteenth chapter of First Corinthians (see www.dickb.com, *A.A.'s Roots in the Bible*). The hand of God was moving in my life so fast. God relieved me from the addiction the night I called for help. When I read the book *The Sermon on the Mount*, I found out that Jesus was the only way to our Almighty God. I wept from the very depth of my being throughout the entire book. I knew I was reading the truth for the first time in my life as I was being drawn into a confidence and faith in the Divine. There is more after death than just a slow ride in a hearse!

Now I want to share with you how my divine appointment came about with Barney Z. I was raised in Gig Harbor, Washington. Barney lived in Tacoma, Washington, and was instrumental in starting one of the first A.A. meetings in Gig Harbor in the late 1950s. The meeting was just about two blocks from where I lived, and I walked the same ground he had many times past the church where the meetings were held. Barney Z. also was instrumental in starting and attending the A.A. meeting at the Western State Hospital on the Criminally Insane Ward that met every Thursday evening. I also walked the same ground he had many times to and from that ward.

So here is the bigger picture. By the 1970s, my brother had been vacationing at juvenile centers, and I was in Cincinnati, Ohio, just starting my drinking career. After becoming an unwed mother, I married a man from back home and returned to Washington. My brother was now in jail awaiting sentencing. Instead of prison, he was sent to the Western State Hospital for three years as a result of drugs and alcohol. I was well on my way to being a daily drinker by this time. When my brother got out of the hospital, he did not come around the family (or me) very much. I know today he avoided us because it was hard for him to be in a family full of un-recovered people.

Years passed, and now I was a full-blown alcoholic with full drinks on my nightstand. The best thing I could think of then was to apply for a promotion and move. I left for Yuma, Arizona, on a promotion. I was there nine months and ended up in the rooms of A.A. with Barney Z. from Tacoma, Washington. I had a divine appointment to go to Yuma and get the book *The Sermon on the Mount*, which would change my life forever. Later I would come to know Barney Z. as the topic controller. He did not tolerate foolishness and deviating from the program. After several years, Barney left Yuma to return to Tacoma. Several more years passed, and I returned to Gig Harbor to start my life over, having endured the darkest days of my life, in recovery (detailed in chapter seven).

By God's mercy (He spared me from what I deserved) and God's grace (He gave me what I did not deserve) I was released from my addiction through my prayer of repentance. I became amazed at the simplicity and effectiveness of this One Day at a Time program. "Take therefore no thought for the morrow: for the morrow shall take thought for the things of itself. Sufficient unto the day is the evil thereof" (Matthew 6:34, KJV). The program seems to work miracles in those who find *It*. Chapter five, page sixty-three of The Big Book of Alcoholics Anonymous reads, "As we felt new power flow in, as we enjoyed peace of mind, as we discovered we could face life successfully, as we became conscious of His presence, we began to lose our fear of today, tomorrow and the hereafter. We were reborn." The reborn here is referring to a spiritual rebirth. Today I can relate the following scripture in direct relationship to the above quotation from The Big Book. "Jesus Christ is the same yesterday and today and forever" (Hebrews 13:8, NIV). Get the revelation!

Concentrate on the present. Living in the present must be the focal point for all living. In the present, I can tell that devil to go! By living one day at a time I can bring life down to a size I can handle. This is even more necessary for the addicted person, because addicted people have a dreaming and planning personality. Addicted people have a habit of reliving the past and of looking to the future. As a believer, I must stay in the present moment and declare and decree the following: "Therefore, I take unto myself the whole armor of God that I may be able to withstand in the evil day, and having done all, to stand. I stand, therefore, having my loins girt about with truth. Your Word, Lord, which is truth, contains all the weapons of my warfare, which are not carnal, but mighty through God to the pulling down of strongholds" (based on Ephesians 6:10–20).

STUDY EXCERPT: "Half measures availed us nothing. We stood at the turning point. We asked His protection and care with complete abandon."

That moment of letting go of the old self is a dreadful moment. The experiences by which we reach the turning point are themselves awful, and at the very moment of that turning point we may decide our life and our eternity. This turning point is where we are uncertain of the future, and if we do not make a decision to move, despair will overwhelm us. Our past experiences of failure and loss will feed our present response and rise up like a giant. When we do choose to move forward, from that moment on we will never be the same. By the time you get to the Third Step of the Twelve Step Program, you will have to make this choice with complete abandon.

During my drinking career, as long as a problem pressed for a solution and I chose to keep it unsolved, it tore at my whole personality even though I might not have been consciously thinking of the problem. I continued to be indecisive about what was causing havoc in my life and the life of my family. I procrastinated while I was in my hurts, habits, and hang-ups, and then quit thinking about the problem on a regular basis— only to start up thinking about the problem again. So my problems increased, and I grew a thicker armor, always resisting the tough solution. My well-rooted habit of procrastination had developed a stronghold in me. This repeated behavior caused my tension, irritability, anxiety, and depressive moods—all as a result of the conflict going on inside of me.

My soul made little or no progress toward the practice of honesty or finding a relationship with God before I entered recovery. I would quit drinking frequently and make a lot of noise doing it. Then, I would just dig up another excuse to cover the neglect that came from my habit of indecision.

Here's an example of my endless quitting pattern. My three children were at home as I made my great announcement again that, "I am going to quit drinking!" I had taken all the booze out of the house again and thrown it in the dumpster just outside the house. At that time I never could bring myself to pour it down the sink. My oldest son said, "What did you do, mom?" I replied, "I quit, and there are going to be some changes in this house." My son had a smile on his face from ear to ear. Little did I know my children really did look forward to my quitting so I could change my ways. Then they and their friends would proceed to retrieve the booze from the dumpster again for a night of partying. All I can say is that my thinker was broken.

While standing at that turning point, the morning I finally called for help, I asked the living God for His protection and care with complete abandon. Not knowing what was happening to me, I still took that step of faith. Later I could identify that I had a divine appointment with God in my surrender that day. I turned from a physical dependency to a spiritual dependency. Then a healing process began. The transformation that took place was obvious to those around me before I even started working with a sponsor and doing the steps. I did not walk the same, talk the same, or visit the same people and places. One of my co-workers came up to me a few months after I entered the Twelve Step Program and asked me if I was on drugs, because I had had such a significant personality change. A new level of faith had been imparted to me. New challenges came all the time, but I was being moved from new faith levels to new faith levels and from glory to glory.

I remember as a child hearing sayings like, "The road to hell is paved with good intentions." So it must be that the half measures availed nothing. So it must be that the road to heaven is paved with full measures. Amen.

STUDY EXCERPT: "Here are the steps we took, which are suggested as a program of recovery:"

Suggested! No one could make me do this program, and I found out that no one would, either. I found it interesting that the word "suggested" is synonymous with "optional" and "recommended." So, if I wanted what those in the program had, I would have to be willing to go to any length to get it, or I would miss the miracle. The word "recovery" is synonymous with "renewal" and "revival." Later I would recognize that I had started my own *revival* in me!

One Thursday evening I had gone to a meeting at a very large church where we met in the church's library and general purpose room. That particular night I saw a book on the library shelf. What caught my eye were the words "healing" and "faith" on the book cover. The name of the book was *The Healing Power of Faith*, by Will Oursler. Immediately, I got up from my chair and pulled the book out to peruse the table of contents. I saw the chapter titled "Healers Anonymous." I said to myself, "Oh no, not another anonymous program!" My sponsor was sending me to every Twelve Step Program there was to deal with all the pain I carried. The author chose the phrase Healers Anonymous to describe his analysis of the interview he had with Bill W., co-founder of The Alcoholics Anonymous Program. Will Oursler was a versatile and prolific writer and was called a renaissance (synonym for revival) man in the 1930s. He started his writing career at Harvard as a student correspondent for the Hearst papers in Boston. He graduated from Harvard *cum laude* in 1937. His first book was published by Simon and Schuster in 1941. In 1957, Will Oursler published the book *The Healing Power of Faith*, which documented miraculous healing processes around the world.

This book gave me confirmation that I was in the right place and was on a real spiritual journey. Yes, it was a miracle! I had a divine appointment to pick that book off the library shelf out of hundreds and hundreds of books.

This is what I read that night. From chapter twenty-seven, page 257, of the *Healing Power of Faith* by Will Oursler:

That Alcoholics Anonymous is, in fact, an organization devoted exclusively to spiritual healing is frequently overlooked. There are no crutches left on the walls of an A.A. meeting hall that are visible to the naked eye. There are no religious services or rituals as such, no laying on of hands or anointing.

Yet the first three steps of the Twelve Steps in A.A. bring in factors which are a process of transfer, from physical to spiritual concepts. Here are these first three steps as given in A.A. pamphlets:

STEP ONE: We admitted that we were powerless over alcohol—that our lives had become unmanageable.
STEP TWO: We came to believe that a Power greater than ourselves could restore us to sanity.
STEP THREE: We made a decision to turn our will and our lives over to the care of God as we understood Him.

Thus the break comes with medical and psychiatric treatment. Medicine and psychiatry admit that alcoholism is a disease, or as some call it, the symptom of a deeper disease of mind or psyche. But medicine does not usually write prescriptions involving God.

On the other hand doctors and psychiatrists, concerned with helping people get well, and entirely pragmatic, willingly accept A.A. as a valuable tool in many cases, metaphysical concepts and all. It is a paradoxical situation, unique in the history of modern medicine.

STEP ONE

STUDY EXCERPT: "Step One: We admitted we were powerless over alcohol—that our lives had become unmanageable."

The First Step in the Twelve Step Program is as honest as it gets. It must be a 100 percent honest admission in order for a person to start recovery and remain in recovery. A great deal of humility is required to make this admission, and many people are skilled at finding excuses that will allow them to avoid taking this step. Again, I will say that every person on the road to recovery must face that dreaded moment when we must see ourselves for who we are and what we have done. In the *Golden Books* authored by Father John Doe (anonymous) in 1963, he revealed that to most of us this dreaded moment came when life was passing us by. It came to us while we were consumed with fighting everybody and everything, but God gave so many of us sufficient years to seek the truth and pursue *How It Works* and to make *It* the motive of living out the principles of the program one day at a time.

So for most of us, admission comes at the instant when we face the inevitable choice of death and insanity, or emotional sobriety. What describes this turning point for me today is the way of the prodigal son, who dropped on his knees in the pig pen and cried, "Father, I have sinned!" or "I am powerless; my life is unmanageable. God, help me!" I personally fell to my knees in that pig pen and cried out, "God help me!" on October 14, 1987.

Perhaps for the first time in our lives, we prodigals pray and begin to meditate. We are humbled. Day by day we pray and we meditate on the truth for fear we again will fall back into former dishonesties, into our former self-deception, and into our former life-long habit of excuses in the pig pen. I have found that this is where the rooms of the Twelve Step Programs have opened their arms and received the prodigals such as me back into the bosom of life, where many times the family does not receive them. Then Mercy walks in!

Step Two

Study Excerpt: "Step Two: We came to believe that a Power greater than ourselves could restore us to sanity."

To be restored to sanity must mean we were once sane and have fallen away from sanity. If we have been insane or are neurotic there comes a whole new battery of excuses that get us into trouble. I will never forget, while in my drinking career, I was diagnosed with angioedema (a swelling of the tissues around the mouth or of the lower layers of the skin, especially on the hands), as well as anxious, neurotic behaviors. The angioedema had become life threatening as I was in and out of hospitals and doctors' offices, getting lots and lots of prescriptions. Immediately after my divine appointment with and surrender to God that first morning when I called for help, the angioedema and neurotic illnesses I had been diagnosed with were gone. I had lost my fear of today, tomorrow, and the hereafter.

This is the plight of the disillusioned and disheartened. There are walls of indifference and prejudice surrounding us. Addicted people are full of contempt prior to investigating change. Defiance is an outstanding characteristic of these addicted people, who are full of bitterness and unforgiveness.

The most pitiful case I was ever exposed to was a young girl in her late twenties or early thirties. She was released from prison and had come to my home, which was then a halfway house for women called Community House. She just couldn't get it together. The lusts of this world powerfully seduced her back. Working the steps and getting honest was not working for her. She left the house and hooked up with lesbians who were acquaintances from prison. She chose death.

Several years passed, and I left Yuma for a new job. I went around and said goodbye to many people at many different meetings. I knew of the trailer park where Amy (not her real name), the woman who had stayed at my house, was living. I went there and tried to say my goodbyes to her. Amy lived with a woman named Beth, and Beth was singing the same song I had heard Amy sing when she first got out of prison. Beth was going to get straight and get her kids back. Amy was the one I wanted to see, and she was in another trailer in the same park. I was told that I might not recognize her. I went to that other trailer, but she would not answer the door. I heard her move around inside, but she was not going to open the door. I said that I loved her and directed her back to the Twelve Step Program as I finished up talking through the door. I could see that her hope had been destroyed. But as long as an addicted person is breathing, a miracle can still happen for them. How low do we have to go before we get It? "The thief does not come except to steal, and to kill, and to destroy. I have come that they may have life, and that they may have it more abundantly" (John 10:10, NKJV). Choose life!

Step Two becomes the turning point to a right relationship with God. To complete this step you only have to stop fighting everybody and everything, even God. Chapter five, page sixty-two of The Big Book says, "God is our Father, and we are His children." God now becomes the Director of our lives. "I will give you a new heart and put a new spirit within you; I will take the heart of stone out of your flesh and give you a heart of flesh. I will put My Spirit within you and cause you to walk in My statutes, and you will keep My judgments and do them. Then you shall dwell in the land that I gave to your fathers; you shall be My people, and I will be your God" (Ezekiel 36:26–28, NKJV). This concept gives us the right of passage through the new and triumphant arch through which we passed to freedom. All sorts of remarkable things begin to happen. We don't talk the same, walk the same, or go to the same places with the same people. More and more we become interested in seeing what we can contribute to life. We feel new power flow in, we enjoy peace of mind, we uncover the truth about God, and we can face life successfully. We become conscious of His presence and we begin to lose interest in ourselves. We are reborn! We were now at Step Three.

STEP THREE

STUDY EXCERPT: "Step Three: We made a decision to turn our will and our lives over to the care of God as we understood Him."

Humility is the most basic of all the virtues. Any other virtue is impossible without humility. Emotional sobriety is impossible without humility. It is acquired not by talk but by action, with a deep conviction that all depends on our relationship with God. All that I am, all that I have, all that I ever hope to be has been given to me by Almighty God. At this step I had become willing to be dependent upon God.

A familiar phrase heard around the rooms of recovery is, "but for the grace of God." It is used over and over again, because we have all realized that the entire Twelve Step Program has been by the grace of God. From the second step through the entire program, each success and every victory is the result of God's mercy (God's ability to keep from us what we deserve) and grace (God's ability to give us what we do not deserve).

When we make up our minds to turn our will and lives over to the care of God, we must do so without reservation. Therefore all dishonesty, dishonest practices, illicit relationships, and all the things in our lives that we know are contrary to the will of God must go. It is here that we understand fully the meaning of the term unconditional surrender. Now having once and for all fully made this decision of surrender, we will, perhaps for the first time in our lives, experience the true meaning of peace and serenity. We will finally begin to live. We shall at last understand what Christ meant when He told us that we must die in order to live, die to all that is of self in order to live to all that is of God. His will—not mine—be done. The ego must be smashed every day. Ego stands for Edging God Out.

"As we understood Him": We are above everything else searching for the truth about life and our purpose. Therefore, we don't make up a God to fit us, but we search for God according to our honest convictions. We want the God who can restore us to sanity, and who is a power greater than ourselves, not a figment of our imagination or a product of our own will. If we have no clear cut idea of God, we should ask that He give it to us. Isn't it clear that the making of a God to suit us is a contradiction of the admission we make that we were powerless? The safe and sure way is to humbly pray and ask God to see. "Ask, and it shall be given to you; seek and ye shall find; knock, and it shall be opened unto you" (Matthew 7:7, KJV).

Bill Wilson's wife Lois (Bill Wilson is one of the co-founders of A.A.) documented that it was agreed that The Big Book should present a universal spiritual program, not a specific religious one, since all drunks were not Christians. I thought this was so profound the first time I heard it, because there was another saying around the rooms of recovery that confirmed the need for this universal approach. The saying was, "You cannot clean fish before you catch them." Get the revelation! Dr. Bob (the other co-founder of A.A.) mentioned often in historical documents that their ideas for Alcoholics Anonymous came from their study of the Bible. Members began their day with a prayer for strength and a short period of Bible readings. They found the basic messages they needed in the Sermon on the Mount, 1 Corinthians, and the Book of James.

The book of James reveals the Twelve Step recovery process. When I read the Book of James, I feel conviction. It is a book I need to read often, not only for the conviction but for the confirmation of this Twelve Step process. In Jerry Cook's book *Love, Acceptance & Forgiveness*, chapter four, page sixty-three, he writes a very refreshing view of the scriptural Book of James. Cook says, "We read the book of James. I can't preach James. It would beat the people to death. I tried it. The most I could cover preaching through the book of James was about four or five verses and people were bloody all over the floor. I said, 'Oh, man, we've got to call this thing off. James is nailing us to the wall.' I don't need to preach the book of James. I just read it and the Holy Spirit clouts people; it's a heavy book."

Here is the Third Step prayer that many A.A. members have said (chapter five, page sixty-three of The Big Book): "God, I offer myself to Thee—to build with me and to do with me as Thou wilt. Relieve me of the bondage of self, that I may better do Thy will. Take away my difficulties, that victory over them may bear witness to those I would help of Thy Power, Thy Love, and Thy Way of life. May I do Thy will always!" This prayer carries the same anointing yesterday, today, and tomorrow. I remember my sponsor (Judy J.) said to me, "Okay, you are ready, come with me." She took me into her living room, got two pillows for us to kneel on, and we said this prayer together. I just remember how there was a moaning coming from me as she held me up and I cried all the way through it. She kept telling me I had to say it out loud. There is truly something miraculous that happens when a prayer is said out loud with holy conviction, as doubt and unbelief subside.

If one means every word of this prayer, one must now acknowledge what is written in the Book of Matthew when John baptizes Jesus:

Then Jesus came from Galilee to John at the Jordan to be baptized by him. And John tried to prevent Him, saying "I need to be baptized by You, and are You coming to me?" But Jesus answered and said to him, "Permit it to be so now, for thus it is fitting for us to fulfill all righteousness." Then he allowed Him. When He had been baptized, Jesus came up immediately from the water; and behold, the heavens were opened to Him, and He saw the Spirit of God descending like a dove and alighting upon Him. And suddenly a voice came from heaven, saying, "This is My beloved Son, in whom I am well pleased."

MATTHEW 3:13-17, NKJV

We may either put our faith in ourselves, or in our attachments, or in God. It is that simple. At this point, if anyone still has a reservation or is still balking at this surrender to God's will, I say to you, "Go back to step one, because you are still wallowing in the pig pen; or go back to step two, because you are still fighting. Going on would be fruitless for you time and time again. Or you can purchase the book *The Sermon on the Mount*, by Emmet Fox, which was used by the co-founders of the Twelve Step Program, and I would recommend you read it until you understand that Jesus was, is, and will always be the only way to the Father. He intercedes for us every minute of every day. "Jesus saith unto him, I am the way, the truth, and the life: no man cometh unto the Father, but by me" (John 14:6, KJV). Choose life!

Bill's Story in The Big Book, in chapter one, page thirteen to fourteen, says, "Belief in the power of God, plus enough willingness, honesty and humility to establish and maintain the new order of things, were the essential requirements. Simple, but not easy; a price had to be paid. It meant destruction of self-centeredness. I must turn in all things to the Father of Light who presides over us all." Read that last sentence again. Bill refers to the Father of Light. Now listen to yourself read John 8:12 (KJV, emphasis mine): "Then spake Jesus again unto them, saying, *I am the light* of the world: he that followeth me shall not walk in darkness, but shall have the light of life." Bill is telling you about Jesus, the son of God! The scales must now fall off of your eyes so that you can see this power greater than yourself. Choose life!

Have you heard of the Four Spiritual Laws? This is the name of a booklet written by Bill Bright. The laws are:

1) God loves you and offers a wonderful plan for your life.
2) Man is sinful and separated from God. Therefore, he cannot know and experience God's love and plan for his life.
3) Jesus Christ is God's only provision for man's sin. Through Him you can know and experience God's love and plan for your life.
4) We must individually receive Jesus Christ as Savior and Lord; then we can know and experience God's love and plan for our lives.

Through all my reading and studying of the Bible, volumes of books, videos, programs, and more, the most important revelation I got was that if I did not accept Jesus Christ as my savior while I cannot see Him, someday when I do see Him, He will not be my Savior; He will be my Judge! "And then I will declare to them, 'I never knew you; depart from Me, you who practice lawlessness!'" (Matthew 7:23, NKJV). Alcohol, drugs, pornography, and gambling are all rooted in lawlessness and all bear fruits of lawlessness. Do not be deceived by the shift of *sociably acceptable*. Choose life!

How To Be Born Again by Billy Graham was published in 1977. Billy Graham said the expression "born again" was not a new term, invented by modern journalists. The term was given to us by Jesus. Jesus said to one of the intellectuals who had come to him for answers, "I say to you, unless one is born again, he cannot see the kingdom of God" (John 3:3, NKJV). As I was seeking answers to my questions, I devoured the words Billy Graham wrote about the need for a spiritual transformation. Since I was a spiritual wasteland I knew it was something I could not do for myself. I had already chased all sorts of cures for feeling better. I searched for *It* in drugs, alcohol, but all of these methods lead to a spiritual wasteland. Billy Graham explained that only God could give me the new birth I so desperately wanted and needed. He translated all the Christian language that I was hearing and reading about. The bottom line Billy Graham got across to me was that man apart from God is spiritually dead. I needed to be born again and only by God's grace, through faith in Christ, can this new birth take place. Choose life!

"Therefore, if anyone is in Christ, he is a new creation; the old has gone, behold, the new has come!" (2 Corinthians 5:17, NIV). My NIV Study Bible says that this was the Apostle Paul's most characteristic expression of what it means to be a Christian.

Our relationship with Christ affects every aspect of our lives. The most important issue in our lives is about our relationship with Christ, not with religion. When this new birth takes place, it is evident that we have passed through the east gate of the tabernacle on a journey to the presence of God into the Holy of Holies. We came through the works of the Gospels (Matthew, Mark, Luke, and John). We are headed for the brazen altar in the Temple (Step Four) where we will burn off our flesh (ego, pride) and prepare to offer our bodies as living sacrifices to God. This process may take some time. I personally have had to crawl up on that brazen altar more than once.

Everything about your life can change right now! You can receive Christ right now by praying (talking with God). Fall to your knees in your pig pen and cry out, "God, help me! Lord Jesus, I need You. I believe You died on the cross for my sins and You were raised from the dead. I open the door to my heart to receive you as my Lord and Savior. Take control of my spirit, soul, and body. Make me that person that you want me to be."

That is it! You just put a smile on His face. The angels are rejoicing for you. Your name has been written in the Lamb's Book of Life. You are a new creation! This is your gift of mercy and grace.

You should thank God often that Christ is in your life and that He will never leave you. "Let your conduct be without covetousness; be content with such things as you have. For He Himself has said, 'I will never leave you nor forsake you'" (Hebrews 13:5, NKJV). When you don't know what to pray, just say His name: "Jesus." Find a Bible-based church to attend so you can grow and thrive in the word of God. Continue now through the steps, always remembering He is with you. Just call on Him and become an "old-timer." Keep going back to your Twelve Step Programs to be a sponsor to those who will be coming after you. Choose life!

These first three steps of the Twelve Step Program are about relationship-building with God through His son Jesus Christ. We need to become dependent upon God as we launch out on a course of vigorous action, which is our personal housecleaning. The purpose of cleansing is for preparation, so that something may follow. Note that the first three of the Ten Commandments are about our relationship with God. The rest of the Commandments are about our relationship with man. The first three of the Twelve Steps are about our relationship with God. The rest of the Steps are about our relationship with man. Get the revelation!

Step Four

Study Excerpt: "Step Four: We made a searching and fearless moral inventory of ourselves."

Once you have surrendered to God by the way of the cross, you can really get the action going. The words "searching" and "fearless" mean to carefully explore inside ourselves, without fear of whatever we may find, leaving no nook or cranny of ourselves, past or present, unsearched. Remember you were already forgiven; now just receive it into your heart! The goal at this point is to discover all of the defects of character in yourself that God already knows about.

You must first explore the wreckage of your past. In order to clear up the wreckage of the past, you must first stop making more wreckage in the present. And you can't make up an imaginary list to work on, either. This is to be an honest list, and it may take some time.

I personally found that my children often reminded me of things to put on my list. I had put my two younger children in a drug and alcohol and mental treatment facility for adolescents. I was given the opportunity to be confronted with all of their memories, distorted or not. They gave me a thorough report of what happened to them as a result of my addictions. In taking my inventory, I had no choice but to accept what they had to say. I was a black-out drinker, and as my memories of those times are very unclear, I had no choice but to believe what they told me. What would I have really known for sure? I walked through treatment for thirty days with my son and for ninety days with my daughter. I kept my holy conviction that the outcome of this too depended on God, as I prayed for God's will for all of us.

Christ has told us, "If you love Me, keep My commandments" (John 14:15, NKJV). Again, remember that the first three commandments are about our relationship with God and the rest of the commandments are about our relationship with man. The commandments are the basis of the moral law, so in taking a moral inventory of ourselves, we learn wherein we have failed to love Him and our neighbor. "He who loves his brother abides in the light, and there is no cause for stumbling in him. But he who hates his brother is in darkness and walks in darkness, and does not know where he is going, because the darkness has blinded his eyes" (1 John 2:10–11, NKJV).

This is where the sponsor should come into your recovery process. Stick to the process provided in the Twelve Steps. Look for the old-timer in the program. The story of the ten lepers is a unique picture of what you should be seeking in a sponsor, and that should be gratitude! The story of the ten lepers goes like this:

> Now it happened as He went to Jerusalem that He passed through the midst of Samaria and Galilee. Then as He entered a certain village, there met Him ten men who were lepers, who stood afar off. And they lifted up their voices and said, "Jesus, Master, have mercy on us!" So when He saw them, He said to them, "Go, show yourselves to the priests." And so it was that as they went, they were cleansed. And one of them, when he saw that he was healed, returned, and with a loud voice glorified God, and fell down on his face at His feet, giving Him thanks. And he was a Samaritan. So Jesus answered and said, "Were there not ten cleansed? But where are the nine? Were there not any found who returned to give glory to God except this foreigner?" And He said to him, "Arise, go your way. Your faith has made you well."
>
> LUKE 17:11-19, NKJV

Ingratitude did not deny Christ's mercy to the other nine, but ingratitude did deprive them of fellowship with Him. Around the rooms of recovery I always heard sayings like, "Only one out of ten of us are going to make it." I used to say, "Where do they get their statistics for this?" Little did I know that the story of the ten lepers has driven those statistics since the beginning of the Twelve Step Program. Get grateful and choose life!

The old-timers keep coming back, because they know the rewards of giving and being grateful. They know they have been called to be a sponsor. "These twelve Jesus sent out and commanded them, saying, 'Do not go into the way of the Gentiles, and do not enter a city of the Samaritans. But go rather to the lost sheep of the house of Israel. And as you go, preach, saying, "The kingdom of heaven is at hand." Heal the sick, cleanse the lepers, raise the dead, cast out demons. Freely you have received, freely give'" (Matthew 10:5-8, NKJV). You will be able to see the fruit of the old-timer. Find that grateful person, and you will find a humble person with experience, strength, and hope freely given.

Gratitude is a frequent topic in meetings around Thanksgiving. But if you have to wait for the arrival of a turkey to get you to talk about gratitude, you might see why so many members are in trouble. Here is an idea to start you on the road to gratitude. Go through the alphabet and make a gratitude list periodically for the small stuff as well as the unexplainable favor (act of kindness, preference, increase) given to you. At my original home-group meeting, Friday was always the topic of gratitude. In my early recovery I frequently found that after listening to others and their struggles I would feel really grateful to leave the meeting with my own relatively small problems. Later my gratitude grew in every area of my life.

It has always been suggested that the inventory be physically written, and this indicates the value of action. When sincerity in the making of the list is present, then the action takes place in the next step. All of us missed the mark; there is not one person who is capable of fulfilling all of God's laws at all times. In our spiritual lives we are constantly falling. There is no way we can turn in a perfect performance. This is why we claim spiritual progress, not perfection. Keep going. We have not reached sainthood yet!

When there is still unrest and questioning comments in us, such as "something just seems missing in my program," or "I can't seem to grasp this," or "some people have serenity which I haven't got," this means that you have not made a full decision with no reservations, no holding back, no cutting of corners, to turning your life over to the care of God. You need to go back to Step Three. You are still hanging on to self and rebelling. The cause of rebellion is "the lust of the flesh, the lust of the eyes, and the pride of life" (1 John 2:16, NKJV). You are still fighting. Going on to the next step would be fruitless and painful. This must be an honest inventory.

STEP FIVE

STUDY EXCERPT: "Step Five: We admitted to God, to ourselves, and to another human being the exact nature of our wrongs."

Many have admitted their wrongs to God and to themselves for years. That admission was easy. It required no action, no change, and no effort. It simply remained mental. If we are honest in taking this fifth step, the nature of its action will allow us to take the next step, and the next step, and so on. Step five begins a new kinship (relationship, affiliation, understanding) with God. "And the prayer of faith will save the sick, and the Lord will raise him up. And if he has committed sins, he will be forgiven. Confess your trespasses to one another, and pray for one another, that you may be healed. The effective, fervent prayer of a righteous man avails much" (James 5:15-16, NKJV).

Your sponsor will help you to come to grips with pride, lust, anger, and resentments. Confession is an ancient discipline. The sponsor will help you look at these things in your home life, in your social life, in your business life, in your financial affairs, in your spiritual life, in your emotional life, in your physical life, and in your mental life. You don't just confess the failures; you show God how serious you are about changing (repenting).

Consider also your inventory on how we so grieved the Lord directly. In the book *Time to Weep* by Stephen Hill, there is a statement on the power of repentance that brings revival. He lays out the following truths:

1) We grieved the Lord by not knowing His ways and by neglecting His great work of atonement on the cross.

2) We also grieve the Lord by our disobedience.

3) We cause the Lord sorrow by denying His presence.

4) We cause the Lord sorrow by having idols in our lives.

A good self-examination and confession of our prideful attitude is always in order. This is a time to weep! Repent!

The sponsor will also help you look at these areas in your recovery life. Dissension in recovery groups in the form of slips, gossip, slander, splits, and the like all stem from resentments. Such group problems are an opportunity to practice patience, kindness, and tolerance. But the day will come when enough is enough and action must be taken in love to edify God.

This is also where the saying "easy does it" comes in. It was probably the first principle I heard in the rooms of all the recovery arenas I have attended. This is the principle that will enable the sensitive, stubborn, and perfectionist recovery member to learn to handle pressure, tension, and opposition in everyday living without resorting to old habits. The rest of the saying is "but do it" when it is to be done. So we begin to learn patience, acceptance, tolerance, and thoroughness without hurry and without procrastination. Get with a sponsor to clean house and serve God. There is a miracle in your house—don't give up before you see it. Remember, we left Egypt, and we are now headed for the Promised Land.

STEP SIX

STUDY EXCERPT: "Step 6: We were entirely ready to have God remove all these defects of character."

If we were honest in taking the Fifth Step, then it demands that we get ready to remove what we have admitted were our wrongs, faults, and failures. Self-enforced obedience to the word of God brings calmness on the outside for others to see. After digging up the good, the bad, and the ugly, we find a pleasant relief to acknowledge that God already knew about our past. Who were we kidding? Only by sharing our inventory with another human being, even our go-to-the-grave secrets, and accepting direction could we begin the spiritual transformation, through honesty and genuine humility.

Now you are ready for God to remove the mania of the abundance of our natural desires, which we let far exceed their intended purpose.

STEP SEVEN

STUDY EXCERPT: "Step Seven: We humbly asked Him to remove our shortcomings."

We can't just admit our faults and then not do anything about them. If we did nothing at this point, it would be rebellion against God's Word. Many have loudly petitioned God to take away their pride, but they make no concentrated effort to practice humility. There is no way to hide the lack of humility. Repentance must come so that humility is experienced. We must truly eliminate pride in ourselves, not just talk about doing so. Self-enforced obedience to God's Word brings serenity within. Humbly ask God for help. I can go boldly to the throne of God, because I am forgiven. "Let us therefore come boldly to the throne of grace, that we may obtain mercy and find grace to help in time of need" (Hebrews 4:16, NKJV). "Coming boldly" literally means without reservation and with frankness. We approach a throne of grace, not of judgment, obtaining mercy for the past and grace for the present and future.

It is at this point that my sponsor helped me understand forgiveness. Before I could truly deal with the harm I had caused through my shortcomings, I needed to deal with the forgiveness for the harm that was done to me. I was oozing with pain as a wounded child, an adult child of alcoholics, and a codependent.

I had a spiritual experience at the close of a meeting one night when we were all holding hands and saying The Lord's Prayer. The women who shared at the meeting that night literally told my story. There was a weighty heaviness that came over me as she spoke. Next we were praying, and, as is the case every time I prayed, I kept my eyes closed so I could better concentrate on every word I was hearing. This night while my eyes were closed, the words "Our Father" lit up on the inside of my eyelids. The word "Our" was on the left lid, and the word "Father" was on the right lid. I could not open my eyes until the prayer was finished. Then I wrote the experience down when I got home. I still felt the heaviness on me as I was going home in total amazement of what I had experienced.

The fact that God is our Father means that He is everyone's Father, and He loves those who have harmed me as much as He loves me. God waits for the day that they will come to Him, just like He was waiting for the day that I came to Him. "Beloved, do not avenge yourselves, but rather give place to wrath for it is written, 'Vengeance is Mine, I will repay,' says the Lord" (Romans 12:19, NKJV). I realized those people would have to answer to God for what they had done to me. God had forgiven me for what I had ever done. If the people who hurt me never come to Christ to be born again, it is none of my business to monitor them. But to pray for the will of God for them is my business.

When I forgive someone, I pray in the following manner, for I know that I could not forgive him or her on my own: "Father, as You have forgiven me I forgive _____ for _____."

It makes the forgiveness final, and I feel as if I can move on. Pain is the admission price to a new life. Step Seven is about a change in our attitude.

STEP EIGHT

STUDY EXCERPT: "Step Eight: We made a list of all persons we had harmed, and became willing to make amends to them all."

Step Eight deals with direct personal relationships. Chapter six, "Into Action," page seventy-six of The Big Book says, "Learning how to live in the greatest peace, partnership and brotherhood with all men and women, of whatever description, is a moving and fascinating adventure."

No more mental lists. It is now necessary to put it to paper and become willing to deal with this list of people we have harmed. The key word here is being willing. It is at times a painful process to complete the list. Boogeymen we have lived in fear of for years start disappearing as they loose their strength. We must let go of our habit of blaming others and circumstances for our difficulties. Let God help guide you to an honest list of all those who you have harmed with no ands, ifs, or buts left in the list.

STEP NINE

STUDY EXCERPT: "Step Nine: We made direct amends to such people wherever possible, except when to do so would injure them or others."

Now we begin to practice the love of our family and neighbor. We must let go of our pride and lust of the world in this step. By now, you should have a close relationship with your sponsor and understand why we need to smash our ego on a daily basis. Good judgment, timing, and boldness are all qualities we need in order to execute this step. As this step points out, this is no time to be reckless and cause more wreckage in the present. This step is about clearing up and making restitution for the wreckage of our past.

In the past, the word "sorry" was not in my vocabulary. I justified everything. When two of my children were in the treatment center, I began my amends. I admitted my faults and failures as their mother and the effects my addiction had on their lives. I stepped up to the plate as their renewed mother who put them in treatment as part of my amends to them. For the next three years that I had with my children, I did everything I could as a responsible parent to nurture them physically, mentally, and spiritually (whether they liked it or not). So every time they broke the law and I had the evidence, I called 911 and turned them in.

Several years later I took my daughter to a psychiatrist for what I had decided would be the last time. I said this was going to be it. She was still using drugs and needed to be counseled. At the end of the session, the psychiatrist, who had known us for years, told me to get a life. I was such a good codependent. Surprisingly, he did not insult me at all. In fact I looked at him with amazement and said, "Really?"

Next I was trying to visualize what that meant. Get a life! He then said, "If you don't get a life, how is your daughter to understand that it is okay for her to have one?"

I was still amazed at this man telling me to get a life. I realized that my daughter and I had become too entangled in each other's lives in the healing process. But I could not imagine breaking this enmeshment that we had as a family in recovery. It didn't happen for years, but I worked hard at my recovery and spiritual growth that later set us free.

In circumstances we can't change, in instances where serious harm to others is involved, and in cases where restitution is impossible, we place it entirely in the hands of God. This business of restitution may take years, but it is thoroughness, not haste, that counts. This effort of thoroughness may feel like it is costing us a lot. Remember that willingness here is about experiencing the consequences for those costs. A remorseful mumbling is not the answer; action is the answer. As God's people we stand on our feet: we don't crawl before anyone.

To say I was sorry was a new experience for me. Later, after my daughter was out of treatment and we were still on a roller coaster ride every day, I had to leave work because my mind was so consumed with her getting this message so we could move on. I went home on my lunch hour, because I knew she was home from school that day. I woke her up and waited until she was completely aware of my presence. Next, I looked her in the eyes and told her I was saying that I was sorry for the last time. My children all would have loved it if I had tattooed "I am sorry" on my forehead to wear forever. Remember that making amends is meant to be once and for all. Always remember that we are new creations in Christ and Saul became Paul on the road to Damascus. Years later I would regain respect as their mother in recovery, but that doesn't mean they liked me.

There is always a benefit in doing the right thing. Here at Step Nine we find the promises of recovery in chapter six, page eighty-three, of The Big Book. At every meeting I waited for these promises to be read. I longed for them to start appearing in my life, and I wanted every one of them. The following is referred to as The Promises:

If we are painstaking about this phase of our development, we will be amazed before we are halfway through. We are going to know a new freedom and a new happiness. We will not regret the past nor wish to shut the door on it. We will comprehend the word serenity and we will know peace. No matter how far down the scale we have gone, we will see how our experience can benefit others. That feeling of uselessness and self-pity will disappear. We will lose interest in selfish things and gain interest in our fellows. Self-seeking will slip away. Our whole attitude and outlook upon life will change. Fear of people and of economic insecurity will leave us. We will intuitively know how to handle situations which used to baffle us. We will suddenly realize that God is doing for us what we could not do for ourselves.

Step One through Step Nine are about the past. Freedom is at hand. Where are you going to live? If you want a victorious life and the rewards that are available to you, don't be lukewarm about your recovery and your Christian life:

To the angel of the church in Laodicea write: These are the words of the Amen, the faithful and true witness, the ruler of God's creation. I know your deeds, that you are neither cold nor hot. I wish you were either one or the other! So, because you are lukewarm—neither hot nor cold—I am about to spit you out of my mouth. You say, 'I am rich; I have acquired wealth and do not need a thing.' But you do not realize that you are wretched, pitiful, poor, blind and naked. I counsel you to buy from me gold refined in the fire, so you can become rich; and white clothes to wear, so you can cover your shameful nakedness; and salve to put on your eyes, so you can see. Those whom I love I rebuke and discipline. So be earnest, and repent. Here I am! I stand at the door and knock. If anyone hears my voice and opens the door, I will come in and eat with him, and he with me. To him who overcomes, I will give the right to sit with me on my throne, just as I overcame and sat down with my Father on his throne. He who has an ear, let him hear what the Spirit says to the churches."

REVELATION 3:14-22, NIV

The church in Laodicea supplied neither healing for the spiritually sick nor refreshment for the spiritually weary. They were counseled about their worldliness. Christ is depicted knocking on the door of the individual unbeliever's heart, but in context here it is the self-deluded members of the church that are being addressed. Do not be lukewarm about your recovery. Remember that "recovery" is synonymous with "revival"!

Step Ten

STUDY EXCERPT: "Step Ten: We continued to take personal inventory and when we were wrong promptly admitted it."

There are two types of members in recovery. Some are content with the double life, half flesh and half spirit, half self-effort and half grace. I am not content with half measures. I am seeking with my whole heart to know fully what deliverance from sin and the abiding full power for a walk in God's presence is. God help me to be satisfied with nothing less.

We must continue to look at our assets and liabilities on a daily basis, smashing the ego and experiencing humility. In all situations we need self-discipline. When we feel wrong, we need to promptly take an inventory of the moment. Consider pride, envy, greed, lust, gluttony, sloth, and anger as a quick list to run down. There are emotional traps that can flare up and throw us off guard. Personal triumphs can also catch us off guard. There is a paragraph in the Twelve Step Book of Alcoholics Anonymous, on page ninety-two, that sums it all up. Read the following quote over a few times to get the whole implication:

Finally, we begin to see that all people, including ourselves, are to some extent emotionally ill as well as frequently wrong, and then we approach true tolerance and see what real love for our fellows actually means. It will become more and more evident as we go forward that it is pointless to become angry, or to get hurt by people who, like us, are suffering from the pains of growing up.

The following scripture reflects the same message:

When I was a child, I talked like a child, I thought like a child, I reasoned like a child. When I became a man, I put childish ways behind me. Now we see but a poor reflection as in a mirror; then we shall see face to face. Now I know in part; then I shall know fully, even as I am fully known. And now these three remain: faith, hope and love. But the greatest of these is love."

1 CORINTHIANS 13:11-13, NIV

The NIV Study Bible states that God is love and has communicated His love to us and commands us to love one another. Love supercedes any other gift, because it outlasts them all. Long after all sought-after gifts are no longer necessary, love will still be the governing principle that controls all that God and His redeemed people are and do.

Always remember that we inventory our virtues that have been developed through this process of step work. Our virtues are our qualities such as kindness, humility, generosity, truthfulness, and the work ethic we have developed on this spiritual journey. Our inventory represents our actions for the day. We have a daily reprieve from addictions contingent upon our spiritual progress. Praise Him! For this is the day that the Lord has made. At the end of each day, ask for forgiveness before you lay your head down to sleep, and forgive others as God has forgiven you. Our actions today will determine our tomorrow as we truly thank God for the blessings of today and rest with a good conscience.

STEP ELEVEN

STUDY EXCERPT: "Step Eleven: We sought through prayer and meditation to improve our conscious contact with God as we understood Him, praying only for the knowledge of His will for, us and the power to carry that out."

Daily, let us give ourselves to Him as our God. He will prove that what He has done for us in Christ is no more amazing than what He will do in us every day by the Spirit of Christ when we have an ear to hear.

Our past failure was caused by nothing but unbelief. "Stand firm, then, and do not let yourselves be burdened again by a yoke of slavery" (Galatians 5:1, NIV). It is only by faith that we stand, walk, and live. Faith comes by hearing the Word of God. In simple faith we must count on Him to perform what He has spoken.

Across the centuries, there has been considerable practice of meditation and prayer. I found that libraries and places of worship were like treasure chests waiting to be opened for all those who were knocking, seeking, and asking for more of God. An old-timer, by the name of Glen, said to me that when the time was right I would return to church with a new understanding. Two years later, I attended his funeral in the church of my family origin. From the altar Glen had made arrangements to have *A Vision For You* read from page 164 of The Big Book at the end of the service. I was blessed and smiled from ear to ear.

I was lost as to how to pray and meditate. In the *Twelve Steps and Twelve Tradition's* book meetings we would read the prayer of St. Francis of Assisi, which is all about change. It is a prayer designed to relieve a person of the bondage of self. Self is that which must be emptied from us more than any other thing. The manual that outlines the prayer also suggests that a person reread this prayer several times very slowly, savoring every word and trying to take in the deep meaning of each phrase and idea. Because of this rereading in an attempt to absorb a deeper meaning of what I read, I began to understand this process of meditation (contemplation, reflection). After rereading each line, I felt conviction course through me. Godly emptying of self begins at the moment of conviction, and then repentance must come. Daily I die to self. Not only the repenting by conviction, but the application of what I was reading gave me the power and knowledge to carry out God's will.

Over the years in recovery, I have developed two different libraries. The first library holds books about recovery, self help, and literature on seminars I've attended along the way. The second library holds books on a higher level of spiritual progress. It is in this library that I exhausted my search for books on prayer.

I want to share with you what Tommy Tenny wrote in his book, *Prayers of a God Chaser*. You will find The Divine Gateway to Holy Addiction on page forty-five, as follows: "Hunger is a strange condition. When hunger is satisfied, it always seems to return later with even a greater strength. This is especially true of the hunger for God's presence—the one true addiction of the human soul and the only vital life source He created us to crave."

What a statement about addiction. Perhaps this is why the Scriptures say, "Oh, taste and see that the Lord is good" (Psalm 34:8, NKJV). This verse marks the divine gateway to holy addiction and God obsession. The more you stoke the flames of passion for Him, the more passionately hungry you get. Chapter six, page eighty-eight, of The Big Book says: "Faith without works is dead." And from the Bible: "As the body without the spirit is dead, so faith without deeds is dead" (James 2:26, NIV). Get the revelation!

What the NIV Study Bible says about James 2:26 is that faith inevitably calls us forward to action—to the work within faith. After we seek the perfect will of God for our lives or ministry, and often after other doors have remained closed, God opens unexpected doors intended to usher us into His destiny for our lives. When God does this for you, and there is clearly no question that God is opening the door (not you or someone else), move forward. Such signs are directing us along His miraculous pathway and leading us toward His will and purpose. Waiting in His presence eventually leads to recognizing His movement. When God presents a clear, divinely given opportunity, act on it. There should be the absence of fear when this happens.

For example, I decided to act on writing this book on December 26, 2004. I knew the outline and the bottom line of why I wanted to write the book, but it wouldn't come out. I tried several times to expand on it, and it was not coming forth. When I reflect back now, I can see that God had me in a preparation time of six years, beginning in September, 2001. During this time I read new levels of books about Him, listened to preachers preach His Word, ordered videos of seminars and conferences on specific subjects to watch over and over until I extracted every nugget of information I could get from them. I took long-distance classes of Biblical Studies and Bible Prophesy from Liberty University. I did not date during this six-year period. I can see now, looking back, that I was in preparation for what was to come. Aside from this work, I had no outside interests, other than my immediate family, children, and grandchildren. My spiritual hunger for answers had to be fed every day.

Celebrate Recovery Twelve Step Program had been launched at our church in early 2006. By a miracle of God, I was married, after being divorced for twenty-five years, on September 2, 2006. My loving and understanding husband encouraged me to continue in my ministry of *Twelve Step Work* and the writing of this book.

As I started sitting down to work on this book again, there was still something wrong. Then the Lord put the realization in my heart that I was not including Him openly in this book. I was still trying to hint around about His presence, instead of telling *It* like *It* really is. Once I repented for hinting around about Him (the Lord Jesus), the book just flowed and expanded further than I could have ever imagined. Suddenly, I felt boldness and courage in my writing. My vision for this book was crystal clear from that moment on.

In the book *Love, Acceptance & Forgiveness*, Jerry Cook describes clearly that the reason people get bored is that they do not know what they are saved for. They know what they are saved from and what they are saved to but not what they are saved for.

Rick Warren, in his book *The Purpose Driven Life*, reveals that life is really about living for God, not for oneself. This book revealed to me why I had been saved. I will never forget the rush of what felt like warm oil that ran over me when I turned the page and read the title of Day 2, which is *You Are Not an Accident*. I devoured that chapter and reread it over and over again. There is a God who made me for a reason and for this season. "The Lord delights in those who fear him, who put their hope in his unfailing love" (Psalm 147:11, NIV). By the time I got to Day 36, which was the next morning, I was cut loose. I spent time in preparation, and now I am dressed for the occasion. I was made for a mission to carry this message!

STEP TWELVE

STUDY EXCERPT: "Step Twelve: Having had a spiritual awakening as the result of these steps, we tried to carry this message to alcoholics, and to practice these principles in all our affairs."

The Purpose Driven Life also revealed to me on day thirty-six that I was made for a specific mission. My mission in life is a calling to all Twelve Step arenas. I am called to Twelve Step meetings for the unbeliever and the believer. My assignments to Alcoholics Anonymous and Celebrate Recovery groups are all with the same purpose, and that is to carry the message to those who still suffer. There is another way to live.

In Tommy Tenny's book *Chasing God—Serving Man*, you will discover how to have balance in your life between service and worship. The scripture of John 11:1-44 is the record of Lazarus and his two sisters. Mary represents worship, and the other sister, Martha, represents service. So often we get tied up with attending meetings that we don't take the time needed to worship God for ourselves. There seems to be friction between the worship and service personas. Martha had an attitude toward Mary, and that is where the problem comes in. Tommy Tenny says on page forty-nine, "God is blessed when both service and worship bloom in His presence." This revealed to me that if we remove the friction, we become a powerful force for God!

My dear friend Doug M. from my home group speaks so often about finding this balance. Take a moment and re-read the above paragraph considering worship and service. Our lives are full with our families, jobs, meetings, sponsoring, church, school, rest, prayer, and meditation, etc. We must consider all of this on the road to recovery.

Again, I want to repeat that in the book *Love, Acceptance & Forgiveness,* Jerry Cook states so clearly: "They know what they are saved from and what they are saved to but not what they are saved for." Step Twelve tells us we are saved to get this message to the world and become a force for God. "For we are God's workmanship, created in Christ Jesus to do good works, which God prepared in advance for us to do" (Ephesians 2:10, NIV).

Working with others is also known as "ministry work" as well as "Twelve Step Work." It is our calling when we use our abilities to help others receive this restoration program of recovery. This is where we experience the kind of giving that asks for no reward. We sow the message! We carry the message of the spiritual (divine) awakening (beginning)—that there is another way to live, and that way is with dependence upon God through His son Jesus. We have been granted a gift that amounts to a new state of consciousness and being. We are told to burn this idea into the consciousness of every person we can. The only condition is we have a total reliance on God and a clean house. "Do not be deceived: God cannot be mocked. A man reaps what he sows" (Galatians 6:7, NIV).

Now after the fish (newcomer) is caught by your experience, strength, and hope, you can help them start to clean house one step at a time. Get the newcomers out of the rain and into the nurseries (meetings). Then the progress of maturity, stability, and integrity can begin:

> Until we all reach unity in the faith and in the knowledge of the Son of God and become mature, attaining to the whole measure of the fullness of Christ. Then we will no longer be infants, tossed back and forth by the waves, and blown here and there by every wind of teaching and by the cunning and craftiness of men in their deceitful scheming. Instead, speaking the truth in love, we will in all things grow up into him who is the Head, that is, Christ.
>
> EPHESIANS 4:13-15, NIV

Many women came to me early in my sobriety to ask that I sponsor them and work the steps with them. This was a great challenge for me as I personally had many rough edges to wear off while growing out of my self. Jealousy (a Martha and Mary conflict) was a character defect of mine that took some time to overcome. Specifically, jealousy of tall, skinny blondes was deep in me. As a four-foot, ten-inch brunette, I am not joking when I tell you that I felt like God sent every tall skinny blonde in the program to me to sponsor. God knew what I needed and forced my obedience through humility.

I remember one instance of this particularly well. There was a beautiful blonde lady whom I knew needed a sponsor, and I was biting my tongue in hopes that she would not seek me out. But she did, and I agreed to be her sponsor. So I demanded that she be at my home on Saturday to start working these steps at 10:00 A.M. This young and beautiful lady showed up right on time, and we sat on the couch side by side to study the Steps. Within minutes after studying from The Big Book, she was weeping profusely and threw herself across my lap to be held. I put my hand on her back while pulling her hair out of her face full of tears. As I was comforting her in my arms, I tilted my head up and started asking God to forgive me and thanked him for using me. Then I worked on this Martha and Mary conflict problem of mine with my sponsor. And by the way, that beautiful lady never did come back to see me. It was a divine appointment!

I am so privileged by the way God uses me over and over again in this recovery arena. I sow, spreading seeds of the message wherever I can by my experience, strength, and hope. I carry the message to the jails, prisons, and meetings as a speaker and as a sponsor. I may never see the harvest directly. My calling has been to *sow* wherever I can. But the rewards of the harvest are also mine. Get the revelation!

STUDY EXCERPT: "Many of us exclaimed, 'What an order! I can't go through with it.'"

So many times I heard members cry out about their daily moments of temptations and that this program was just too hard for them. I listened carefully as they shared the humiliating and painful pressures of life that they were experiencing. Inside myself, I felt sick thinking that they might not make it. Whenever I said, "Yes, you can do this, so don't give up," I was really talking to myself. "Blessed is the man who endures temptation; for when he has been approved, he will receive the crown of life which the Lord has promised to those who love Him" (James 1:12, NKJV). The promises of this program were the carrots dangling out in front of me as I also went through the day feeling pain from the pressures of life. When my strength ebbed (ran out, faded), I would run back to another meeting to be filled with this power greater than myself, and God never failed to revive me. Jesus said, "My grace is sufficient for you, for my power is made perfect in weakness" (2 Corinthians 12:9, NIV). So I say to you as I have said to myself, "Don't give up!"

> STUDY EXCERPT: "Do not be discouraged. No one among us has been able to maintain anything like perfect adherence to these principles."

Left to my own devices, I could feel discouraged very easily. The accuser would show up in my head, telling me evil things about my past. Flaming darts came at me from every direction as I began changing my life principles to live by. In the past I had never been perfect enough for the world, and now I was being relieved of the guilt of not being perfect enough for God. God loves me, and His Word says He has a plan for my life! "Submit yourselves, then, to God. Resist the devil and he will flee from you" (James 4:7, NIV). Deliverance from oppression is accomplished by submitting ourselves to God, in full obedience to His Word and in complete dependence and trust. The devil comes to kill, steal, and destroy only.

> STUDY EXCERPT: "We are not saints. The point is that we are willing to grow along spiritual lines. The principles we have set down are guides to progress. We claim spiritual progress rather than spiritual perfection."

The NIV Study Bible says that as we draw near God, we bring ourselves into agreement with God's Word and will, rejecting the lies of the adversary (opponent, enemy) and accepting God's promises and evaluation of our situation. As we resist the devil—renouncing his lies and forsaking our own attitude toward sin—we have the given promise of God's Word that the devil will run from us. There is no place of comfort for a demon in the presence of a joyfully submitted believer who has determined to fully embrace the Lord Jesus and abide by His Word. "Come near to God and He will come near to you. Wash your hands, you sinners, and purify your hearts, you double-minded. Grieve, mourn and wail! Change your laughter to mourning and your joy to gloom. Humble yourselves before the Lord, and he will lift you up" (James 4:8–10, NIV).

As I have mentioned before, I attempted to stop drinking many times in my life, and I always made a lot of noise when I did, too. But by the next day I was back doing what I had done before, knowing my sainthood was over. I always wanted everything right now. That is why the phrase "easy does it" became so important to me in relying on the grace of God to give me success in my recovery. As I became willing to grow along spiritual lines, I realized that I would have to put first things first. This meant order in my life. I was so undisciplined. The order of charity in my life would now be for God, myself, and the common good (interest in the mission field and recovery groups), followed by other family, friends, and enemies. I will never apologize to anyone for becoming God-dependent. Now having this new-found faith means I must develop courage always to accept the outcome of God's will. There certainly had to be order in my life, and I found more courage later when my immediate family became my first mission field.

STUDY EXCERPT: "Our description of the alcoholic, the chapter to the agnostic, and our personal adventures before and after, makes clear three pertinent ideas."

In the chapter "More About Alcoholism," page thirty in The Big Book, "We learned that we had to fully concede to our innermost selves that we were alcoholics. This is the first step in recovery. The delusion that we are like other people, or presently may be, has to be smashed." We do not come to read this book by mistake. This is a heavenly scheduled time for alcoholics like us to face reality.

In the chapter, "We Agnostics," page forty-seven in The Big Book, the agnostic needs to ask himself but one short question: "Do I now believe, or am I even willing to believe, that there is a Power greater than myself?"

The agnostic had to stop doubting the power of God.

In the back of The Big Book, page 165, are stories of other people's journeys, and I used them many times when I needed to have a meeting while I was home alone. Study groups with others sharing about their personal adventures were so enlightening, and the discussions brought forth so many revelations. These stories always helped to confirm that I was in the right place, doing the right things for the right reasons.

STUDY EXCERPT: "A. That we were alcoholic and could not manage our own lives."

Our troubles are of our own making and due to our self-will run riot (uprising, revolt). Any life that is run on self-will can hardly be a perfect picture. We have to be fully persuaded that sobriety is not a matter of our willpower.

STUDY EXCERPT: "B. That probably no human power could have relieved our alcoholism."

In the Doctor's Opinion, page xxvi of The Big Book, Dr. Silkworth states: "They are restless, irritable and discontented, unless they can again experience the sense of ease and comfort which comes at once by taking a few drinks—drinks which they see others taking with impunity. After they have succumbed to the desire again, they pass through the well-known stages of a spree, emerging remorseful, with a firm resolution not to drink again. This is repeated over and over, and unless this person can experience an entire psychic change there is very little hope of his recovery. On the other hand—and strange as this may seem to those who do not understand—once a psychic change has occurred, the very same person who seemed doomed, who had so many problems he despaired of ever solving them, suddenly finds himself easily able to control his desire for alcohol, the only effort necessary being that required to follow a few simple rules." So the only relief they have to suggest to alcoholics of our type is total abstinence!

STUDY EXCERPT: "C. That God could and would if He were sought."

Synonyms of "sought" are "wanted," "required," and "hunted." Today I seek Him via sermons, videos, books, CDs, and tapes, college course, ministry work, and fellowship. When you seek God there is evidence for everyone to see that you had sought Him. We become a light in the darkness. "Ask and it will be given to you; seek and you will find; knock and the door will be opened to you" (Matthew 7:7, NIV). Was a spiritual hunger driving me insane? My answer is yes. No doctor could have convinced me that my bottom-line problem was a spiritual hunger, but now I am fully persuaded that this was the case.

My favorite testimony in The Big Book, page 544, is titled "Freedom From Bondage." There were many negative things in my life that hadn't happened yet due to my addictions, but easily could have happened. When I finished reading this particular testimony, I wanted this new life that the testimony described, and I wanted to stop the wreckage in my life. God restored me. God comes to all who honestly seek Him.

Do yourself a favor and please read for yourself. Read! Read! Read! There is a treasure trove of knowledge and wisdom just waiting for you to read. Start with the history of the Twelve Step Program.

Chapter Two

STUDY OF

"THE HOW & WHY OF IT"

STUDY EXCERPT: "This is the how and why of it. First of all, we had to quit playing God. It didn't work. Next, we decided that hereafter in this drama of life, God was going to be our Director. He is the Principal; we are His agents. He is the Father, and we are His children. Most good ideas are simple, and this concept was the keystone of the new and triumphant arch through which we passed to freedom."

"This is" reveals again the present tense about the scheme of life. It means the same for yesterday, today, and tomorrow. Those two beginning words grab my heart each time I read this page. "This is" says there is no other way. Then, the words "first of all" reveal that there must be a beginning to the order about our lives. The word "next" supports that same order of directions. "Hereafter in this drama of life" reveals again the present tense of the order. "Hereafter" means in the future or after this. So after we quit playing God, in the future, God is going to be our Director. "Drama" is such a great word to use here because it represents an exciting performance, which could be a comedy or a tragedy. What has your drama been like without God as the Director?

The principle of First Things First is paramount if we want to achieve happiness. Before sincere recovery occurs we continue to keep the pleasure of the moment as the first thing in our lives. Addictions were first. When we come into recovery we learn that if we are to keep our recovery, we must maintain serenity in our living, and to maintain serenity we must at all times try to put first things first. And God is always first! Step Eleven says, "Praying only for the knowledge of His will for us and the power to carry that out." This is what gives us the primacy (authority, power, domination) of the spiritual. "Let the word of Christ dwell in you richly" (Colossians 3:16, NKJV).

The common good comes next in order. We are but a small part of a greater whole. Our common welfare will come after this step, but our personal recovery depends on unity with the common welfare. Next we must take care of ourselves in body, mind, and soul. If we don't, eventually we won't be any good to God, to our neighbor, or to ourselves.

The last step is putting our families and friends before strangers. In Ephesians, the apostle Paul describes the desperate condition of you and me before the death of Christ: "Remember that at that time you were separate from Christ, excluded from citizenship in Israel and foreigners to the covenants of the promise, without hope and without God in the world" (Ephesians 2:12, NIV). We had no access, no privileges, nor any opportunity for entering into the God consciousness and experiencing the presence of God. But through the sacrifice of Christ at Calvary, everyone has access into an intimate relationship with God through Jesus.

Notice the word "keystone" used in the excerpt above. The synonyms for "keystone" are "bedrock," "source," and "foundation stone." In the Bible where the word "cornerstone" is used, the synonyms are "foundation stone," "keystone," and "basis." "Consequently, you are no longer foreigners and aliens, but fellow citizens with God's people and members of God's household, built on the foundation of the apostles and prophets, with Christ Jesus himself as the chief cornerstone. In him the whole building is joined together and rises to become a holy temple in the Lord. And in him you too are being built together to become a dwelling in which God lives by his Spirit" (Ephesians 2:19-22, NIV).

Jesus said, "I am the way, the truth, and the life. No one comes to the Father except through Me" (John 14:6, NKJV) (the new and triumphant arch through which we passed to freedom). Biblically, this is referred to as the Eastern Gate where we pass into the outer court spiritually. But don't get stuck in the outer court. Go further, press on. Read everything from my suggested book list, including the Bible, and you will be well on your way in knowledge, and you will not perish. Read for yourself. You are in the right place; get the revelation!

In Franklin Graham's book *The Name*, Graham answers the question: Why is it that the name of the Lord Jesus causes such a fuss? Even I could not tolerate anyone using the name of Jesus around me when in my addictions, and that was because of conviction. I was a spiritual wasteland. I shut off people who said His name and ran when I heard His name mentioned, because it only deepened my fear and insecurity about God's love for me. But why is it that when people curse using His Name, hardly anyone complains? If you speak about Him with respect or pray in His Name, some people cry out that they are offended. Is it conviction?

My childhood friend Carol went to the courthouse with me on the final day of my divorce. We sat in the car talking while waiting for the time to pass. All of a sudden Carol said, "Let's pray before we go up there." She took my hand, and I cringed. I felt like a muskrat wanting to chew my arm off. I think back today about the lack of knowledge I was living in and the spiritual wasteland that I had become. I must have been close to the bottom to have a feeling of wanting to chew my arm off. One day we will all stand before Jesus, and either He will be our Savior or He will be our Judge.

We must accept Jesus Christ as the Truth, the Lord of our lives, and repent of all sins (lies, excuses, harm done, sloth, envy, perversion, sexual immorality, overindulging, addictions, etc.). Then the Holy Spirit moves into our hearts. This is known as being saved, born again, reborn. The Lord demands a public acknowledgement of this. He hung on the cross publicly, and we sinned publicly. This power greater than myself must be declared as Jesus Christ; there is no other way to the Father!

STUDY EXCERPT: "We have entered the world of the Spirit. As a Believer, our next function is to grow in understanding and effectiveness. This is not an overnight matter. It should continue for our lifetime."

If one is not a believer, one cannot enter the world of the Spirit. Only God knows our heart. Notice that the writers of The Big Book capitalized the word "Spirit." This capitalization gives the word the reverence it deserves; otherwise it could have been taken as any spirit and not specifically The Holy Spirit.

Clearly they state that this spiritual journey is for our lifetime. Welcome to this journey of celebrating recovery one day at a time.

STUDY EXCERPT: "If we have carefully followed directions, we have begun to sense the flow of His Spirit into us."

I am a believer of "How it Works" (chapter five) put "Into Action" (chapter six). The sentence inserted into the "Promises" on page eighty-three of The Big Book had an impact on me from the first time I heard it read. The sentence is: "Suddenly realize that God is doing for us what we could not do for ourselves," and this sentence needs to be studied. The synonyms for "suddenly" are "unexpectedly," "abruptly," "rapidly," "swiftly," and "out of the blue." What a great word!

God is doing for us what we cannot do for ourselves, because we are, in a sense, babies. We have to get all these babies (newcomers and believers) into the nursery (meetings) so they can receive the words (scripture, testimonies, experience, strength, and hope) to get nurtured and grow spiritually (born anew). Growth means the development of power and authority. The believers have authority over their lives. When they use that authority, they are using the flow of His Spirit. Jesus is the authority! You are in the right place. Get the revelation!

The believer, who thoroughly understands that the power of God is backing him, senses the flow of His Spirit. He can exercise his authority and face the enemy (sin) fearlessly. This power is delegated through the knowledge of the Word. "It teaches us to say 'No' to ungodliness and worldly passions, and to live self-controlled, upright and godly lives in this present age" (Titus 2:12, NIV). This is when we have to take responsibility to do for ourselves what God's Word tells us to do. This is why so many of us get beat up so badly in the spiritual realm. We do not use the power delegated to us and think that God is going to remove obstacles of sin in our way. We have to say no to the devil (by saying no to drugs, porn, alcohol, gambling, gluttony, etc.). Only then does God have us covered. This is a step of faith. The day of reckoning has come when He will not do for us those things we can do for ourselves. Choose life!

"Surely I have calmed and quieted my soul, like a weaned child with his mother; like a weaned child is my soul within me" (Psalm, 131:2, NKJV).

Chapter Three

STUDY OF

"THE PROMISES"

After "How It Works," the Twelve Steps and the Twelve Traditions are normally read at the beginning of a meeting. The "Promises" can be read at any time. The Promises are even called out to be a topic of a particular meeting. The following are the Promises as they are read in the meetings. They are fulfilled at different times for everyone, but they usually are realized in recovery after you have surrendered and begun the step work.

STUDY EXCERPT: "If we are painstaking about this phase of our development, we will be amazed before we are halfway through. We are going to know a new freedom and a new happiness. We will not regret the past nor wish to shut the door on it. We will comprehend the word serenity and we will know peace. No matter how far down the scale we have gone, we will see how our experience can benefit others. That feeling of uselessness and self-pity will disappear. We will lose interest in selfish things and gain interest in our fellows. Self-seeking will slip away. Our whole attitude and outlook upon life will change. Fear of people and of economic insecurity will leave us. We will intuitively know how to handle situations which used to baffle us. We will suddenly realize that God is doing for us what we could not do for ourselves."

Let's look more closely at a few of the words used in the paragraph above.

PAINSTAKING: Synonyms are "thorough," "careful," and "meticulous." In the beginning of "How It Works" we asked you to be thorough from the very start. That means that the detailed instructions of these steps needed to be painstakingly studied and lived out in order to get to this point of humility! "And what do you benefit if you gain the whole world but lose your own soul? Is anything worth more than your soul?"(Matthew 16:26, NLT). By now we have turned from a physical dependency to a spiritual dependency, and a healing process has begun. We have allowed ourselves to change our attitude about life and living. In this phase of our development, our willingness to make amends may or may not benefit the other person or persons, but it benefits us. The Word of God is clear about the need to repent and follow Him. "God paid a high price for you, so don't be enslaved by the world" (1 Corinthians 7:23, NLT). You and I are not slaves of man. We are free by the blood of Jesus. When we accepted Jesus as our Lord and Savior, we were forgiven. Now making our amends is out of love and building new relationships with man. "Don't copy the behavior and customs of this world, but let God transform you into a new person by changing the way you think. Then you will learn to know God's will for you, which is good and pleasing and perfect" (Romans 12:2, NLT). In this world with all its evil and corruption we find that working these steps is a moral process. What God wants from us is to develop a spiritual and moral growth as Christians. This is pleasing to God, not necessarily to us. His will for us is already good and pleasing and perfect. It is in our love of God that we make our amends and experience humility.

DEVELOPMENT: Synonyms are "growth," "training," and "change." Everyone who confesses the name of the Lord must turn away from lawlessness. In this phase of our development we will be amazed in the security of being part of His church. "Be diligent to present yourself approved to God, a worker who does not need to be ashamed, rightly dividing the word of truth" (2 Timothy 2:15, NKJV). The Lord knows those who are intimately acquainted with Him. "But grow in the grace and knowledge of our Lord and Savior Jesus Christ. To Him be the glory both now and for ever. Amen" (2 Peter 3:18, NKJV). Now since we have turned from law-lessness, we still need to be alert concerning deception in sociably accept-able behaviors or we may fall again. We must be secure in our position by God's Word. "Meditate upon these things; give thyself wholly to them; that thy profiting may appear to all" (1Timothy 4:15, KJV). Be diligent in this phase, we beg of you. You will not only save yourself, but you will save your hearers by being His instrument. Share your experience, strength, and hope so that others may find their way.

AMAZED: Synonyms are "astonished," "shocked," and "surprised." Why are we so surprised when God is faithful? "God will do this, for he is faithful to do what he says, and he has invited you into partnership with his Son, Jesus Christ our Lord" (1 Corinthians 1:9, NLT). He may be trusted to do what He has promised to do, and that is to keep us strong unto the end. "You can pray for anything, and if you have faith, you will receive it" (Matthew 21:22, NLT). It comes to many of us as a surprise when unmer-ited favor starts coming our way. As our faith grows, so does our desire for more of these promises. "When they call on me, I will answer; I will be with them in trouble. I will rescue and honor them" (Psalm 91:15, NLT). Whenever the threats of lawlessness may come to us, day or night, it has been proven by all the promises of God that He will be with those who truly love and trust Him.

FREEDOM: Synonyms are "liberty," "independence," and "choice." This freedom is about acknowledging salvation and not just our igno-rance. "And ye shall know the truth, and the truth shall make you free" (John 8:32-36, KJV). A sinner cannot break free from sin by his own strength. "So humble yourselves before God. Resist the devil, and he will flee from you" (James 4:7, NLT). This is a command to humble our-selves and take immediate action in rooting out our sinful attitude of pride. "For the Lord is the Spirit, and wherever the Spirit of the Lord is, there is freedom" (2 Corinthians 3:17, NLT). It is by turning to the Lord that condemnation and the sentence of death is canceled and replaced by the free life-giving grace of Jesus Christ. His Spirit then dwells in us.

HAPPINESS: Synonyms are "contentment," "cheerfulness," and "gladness." Once we have been set free there is a new happiness, which is for many of us unexplainable. "This is the day the Lord has made. We will rejoice and be glad in it" (Psalm 118:24, NLT). We become more contented with recovery and even start laughing at tragic situations that we have gone through. Yes, it is time to rejoice about this new life one day at a time and be happy in it. "But the Holy Spirit produces this kind of fruit in our lives: love, joy, peace, patience, kindness, goodness, faithfulness, gentleness, and self-control. There is no law against these things!" (Galatians 5:22–23, NLT). When the Holy Spirit controls our lives, He produces the fruit of character. We will always reap what we sow. "I have loved you even as the Father has loved me. Remain in my love. When you obey my commandments, you remain in my love, just as I obey my Father's commandments and remain in his love. I have told you these things so that you will be filled with my joy. Yes, your joy will overflow!" (John 15:9–11, NLT). Obedience and love go together. The Christian way of life is to be joyous, so let it show. We are His disciples, ready to carry this message about addictions in a language of love, not condemnation. We are commanded to love each other.

REGRET: Synonyms are "to be sorry," "to be disappointed," and "remorse." Whoever confesses and renounces their sins finds mercy from God. "People who conceal their sins will not prosper, but if they confess and turn from them, they will receive mercy" (Proverbs 28:13, NLT). Here we are not regretting our past, because it is what God is going to use in our testimony as we recover from our dependency and get another chance at life. "But if we confess our sins to him, he is faithful and just to forgive us our sins and to cleanse us from all wickedness" (1 John 1:9, NLT). Our past represents the truth about us. To confess means to agree with God that what He declares wrong is wrong. If we are truly repentant, God keeps forgiving us. Don't be sorry; be glad! "The Lord isn't really being slow about his promise, as some people think. No, he is being patient for your sake. He does not want anyone to be destroyed, but wants everyone to repent" (2 Peter 3:9, NLT). I was forty years old when I came to the Lord. I thank

God He delayed His coming so that I could come to grips with not regretting my past nor wishing to shut the door on it. He needs my testimony. This is our commission to carry this message to the world.

COMPREHEND: Synonyms are "to understand," "to grasp," and "to figure out." We begin to show some intelligence in our daily decision-making. "For the Lord grants wisdom! From his mouth come knowledge and understanding. He grants a treasure of common sense to the honest. He is a shield to those who walk with integrity" (Proverbs 2:6-7, NLT). When we put our trust in God, He will guide us in our decisions about our recovery. "He has showered his kindness on us, along with all wisdom and understanding" (Ephesians 1:8, NLT). Our transformation is blessed by God alone when we recognize our need for Him and surrender. "If you need wisdom, ask our generous God, and he will give it to you. He will not rebuke you for asking" (James 1:5, NLT). Since God is our source for wisdom, ask Him in your daily meditation for help. God speaks to us through the Scriptures. Wisdom is not just acquired information, but it enables us to face our trials.

PEACE: Synonyms are "calm," "freedom from strife," and "reconciliation." Many people around us do not see God at work in our lives. But we know we are under construction! "In peace I will lie down and sleep, for you alone, O Lord, will keep me safe" (Psalm 4:8, NLT). I am now without anxiety, but nothing brings about this kind of peace more than knowing I am in God's mercy and grace. "Deceit fills hearts that are plotting evil; joy fills hearts that are planning peace!" (Proverbs 12:20, NLT). Blessed are the peacemakers. "Better a dry crust eaten in peace than a house filled with feasting—and conflict" (Proverbs 17:1, NLT). A cheerful heart can have a continual feast under any circumstances, but great wealth and turmoil are the ill-gotten treasures of this world.

USELESSNESS: Synonyms are "hopelessness," "pointlessness," and "vainness." The Bible reveals that just people are not content to live but need to have something to live for. "Pride leads to conflict; those who take advice are wise." (Proverbs 13:10, NLT). When pride comes on us, so does shame and guilt and rebellion. "Hope deferred makes the heart sick, but a dream fulfilled is a tree of life" (Proverbs 13:12, NLT). We were sick, and this program gives us a new life fulfilled. "Faith is the confidence that what we hope for will actually happen; it gives us assurance about things we cannot see." (Hebrews 11:1, NLT). Our new faith in God gives us the power to finish the race of life with our heads held high.

SELF–PITY: Synonyms are "shame," "to feel sorry for oneself," "disappointment." The only way to overcome the fierce effects of our sins is to admit our weakness and trust God's Word. "We are pressed on every side by troubles, but we are not crushed. We are perplexed, but not driven to despair. We are hunted down, but never abandoned by God. We get knocked down, but we are not destroyed" (2 Corinthians 4:8–9, NLT). These paradoxes in life reveal that the power within us is of God, not of self, or surely we would be destroyed. "So let's not get tired of doing what is good. At just the right time we will reap a harvest of blessing if we don't give up" (Galatians 6:9, NLT). We will reap what we sow. The positive or negative consequences of our life choices will catch up with us one way or another. "So be strong and courageous, all you who put your hope in the Lord! (Psalm 31:24, NLT). So lift your head and pour out your heart to the Lord, for our reward is the kingdom of heaven!

SELF–SEEKING: Synonyms are "egotistic," "self-centered," and "self-absorbed." The more we focus on ourselves, the less we focus on God and other people. There are times we are very selfish and at other times not so selfish. But in the height of addictions we are very selfish. "When you follow the desires of your sinful nature, the results are very clear: sexual immorality, impurity, lustful pleasures, idolatry, sorcery, hostility, quarreling, jealousy, outbursts of anger, selfish ambition, dissension, division, envy, drunkenness, wild parties, and other sins like these. Let me tell you again, as I have before, that anyone living that sort of life will not inherit the Kingdom of God" (Galatians 5:19–21, NLT). Here is a list of vices to inventory. The indwelling Holy Spirit produces Christian virtues in the believer's life once we surrender and the wreckage of our past is cleared up. "But he will pour out his anger and wrath on those who live for themselves, who refuse to obey the truth and instead live lives of wickedness. There will be trouble and calamity for everyone who keeps on doing what is evil—for the Jew first and also for the Gentile" (Romans 2:8–9, NLT). Here we must understand the difference between believing in God and believing God. We are judged by our believing His Word and our obedience to the Word.

"For wherever there is jealousy and selfish ambition, there you will find disorder and evil of every kind" (James 3:16, NLT). Godly wisdom allows us to rebuild our lives. We live for serving others and building new relationships with God and man. "And we are instructed to turn from godless living and sinful pleasures. We should live in this evil world with wisdom, righteousness, and devotion to God, while we look forward with hope to that wonderful day when the glory of our great God and Savior, Jesus Christ, will be revealed" (Titus 2:12–13, NLT). We obey God because He loves us. He is our source for everything as we trudge this road of happy destiny.

ATTITUDE: Synonyms are "approach," "way of thinking," "mind-set." Here we improve our conscious contact with God, praying only for the knowledge of His will for us and the power to carry that out. "Joyful are those who obey his laws and search for him with all their hearts. They do not compromise with evil, and they walk only in his paths" (Psalm 119:2-3, NLT). These conditions set down by God for those who love Him are not meant as an option! "Keep the commandments and keep your life; despising them leads to death" (Proverbs 19:16, NLT). If we respect His instructions we will be rewarded; if we disrespect His instructions we will pay for it. It is that simple! "Anyone who listens to my teaching and follows it is wise, like a person who builds a house on solid rock. Though the rain comes in torrents and the floodwaters rise and the winds beat against that house, it won't collapse because it is built on bedrock. But anyone who hears my teaching and doesn't obey it is foolish, like a person who builds a house on sand. When the rains and floods come and the winds beat against that house, it will collapse with a mighty crash" (Matthew 7:24-27, NLT). There will always be circumstances beyond our control. Our strength is in God; this is no time for taking chances by not obeying the Word of God.

INTUITIVELY: Synonyms are "instinctively," "spontaneously," and "naturally." As our faith grows, we naturally bring glory to God. "He staggered not at the promise of God through unbelief; but was strong in faith, giving glory to God; and being fully persuaded that, what he had promised, he was able also to perform" (Romans 4:20–21, KJV). Here we are absolutely convinced that God will perform His Word. "Trust in the Lord with all your heart; do not depend on your own understanding. Seek his will in all you do, and he will show you which path to take" (Proverbs 3:5–6, NLT). Here we develop self-assurance as we seek Him in all we do. "The wise are glad to be instructed, but babbling fools fall flat on their faces" (Proverbs 10:8, NLT). This contrasts good and evil. The wise will prosper while the fool will only bring ruin unto himself.

Chapter Four

STUDY OF

"ACCEPTANCE"

This portion of the study on "Acceptance" is a famous paragraph in the chapter titled "Doctor, Alcoholic, Addict" from The Big Book. Looking up verses yourself will help you gain a greater understanding when you read it again. Use any translation of the Bible to look up the following verses. You will see how they apply to the greater scheme of things.

STUDY EXCERPT: "And acceptance is the answer to all my problems today. When I am disturbed, it is because I find some person, place, thing, or situation—some fact of my life—unacceptable to me, and I can find no serenity until I accept that person, place, thing, or situation as being exactly the way it is supposed to be at this moment. Nothing, absolutely nothing, happens in God's world by mistake. Until I could accept my alcoholism, I could not stay sober; unless I accept life completely on life's terms, I cannot be happy. I need to concentrate not so much on what needs to be changed in the world as on what needs to be changed in me and in my attitudes."

ACCEPTANCE: Synonyms are "approval," "tolerance," and "acknowledgement."
Proverbs 12:14
Jeremiah 31:14b
Joel 2:26

ANSWER: Synonyms are "solution," "key," and "way out."
Jeremiah 33:3
Romans 8:28
Romans 8:31

PROBLEMS: Synonyms are "evils," "troubles," and "harms."
2 Corinthians 4:8–9
Psalm 31:7
Psalm 138:7

DISTURBED: Synonyms are "bothered," "worried," and "uneasy."
2 Timothy 1:7
James 1:5
Psalm 119:165

LIFE: Synonyms are "existence," "living," and "time."
Romans 6:23
Ephesians 2:8–9
1 John 5:11-13

CONCENTRATE: Synonyms are "to think," "to focus," and "to give attention to."
Psalm 32:8
Psalm 119:105
Proverbs 3:5-6

This lesson on acceptance confirms that God knows better than all of us that when we live in the answer (scripture) to our problems; the problems go away!

Chapter Five

STUDY OF

"A VISION FOR YOU"

This portion out of the Chapter "A Vision For You" is usually read at the end of a meeting or called out as a topic for a discussion in group meetings. Page 153 of this chapter is not normally read during the meeting, but it is so significant that I will address it here before we get to page 164, which is the famous reading of A Vision For You.

> STUDY EXCERPT: "Then you will know what it means to give of yourself that others may survive and rediscover life. You will learn the full meaning of 'Love they neighbor as thyself.'"

This is where we go from being a taker to becoming a giver. My sponsor responded sharply to a comment I made about not liking a certain meeting because I didn't get anything personally out of that group of people. "My dear brothers and sisters, how can you claim to have faith in our glorious Lord Jesus Christ if you favor some people over others?" (James 2:1, NLT). She told me that I needed to start giving to that group. When we reach higher spiritual levels, we need to start giving ourselves away and sharing our spirituality with others. Give to others as others so freely gave to you. Yes, indeed, it is good when you truly obey our Lord's royal command found in the Scriptures: "Love your neighbor as yourself" (Leviticus 19:18, NLT).

STUDY EXCERPT: "The age of miracles is still with us. Our own recovery proves that!"

The first and greatest *sign and wonder* that recovery had begun to take place in my life was a significant personality change in me. And, believe me, many people wondered about it, too. One of my rival co-workers came up to me a few months later and asked me if I was on drugs. I was not the same person I had been. I did not walk the same, talk the same, dress the same, or go to the same places with the same people. Everything about my life changed. I was a dead woman walking, and suddenly I was raised from the dead. Signs and wonders!

STUDY EXCERPT: "Still you may say: 'But I will not have the benefit of contact with you who write this book.' We cannot be sure. God will determine that, so you must remember that your real reliance is always upon Him. He will show you how to create the fellowship you crave."

A fellowship is being a group of two or more people who come into agreement with a primary purpose of carrying the message of the Good News to others. I was advised to commit to a home group. I went to three to four meetings a day seven days a week and considered them all my home groups. I found a whole host of new friends who were on the same journey, with a common malady. Yes, this was the bright spot of my life. "For where two or three gather together as my followers, I am there among them" (Matthew 18:20, NLT).

STUDY EXCERPT: "Our book is meant to be suggestive only. We realize we know only a little. God will constantly disclose more to you and to us. Ask Him in your morning meditation what you can do each day for the man who is still sick. The answers will come, if your own house is in order. But obviously you cannot transmit something you haven't got. See to it that your relationship with

Him is right, and great events will come to pass for you and count-less others. This is the Great Fact for us."

This paragraph released me into the treasure troves that is suggested in Step Eleven. The Big Book is a textbook, and all textbooks need to be studied, not just read. I found in the archives of The Big Book a list of the books that Dr. Bob (co-founder of A.A.) had read. As I began to find, read, and study the books on this list, God revealed that I was in the right place seeking after Him. God will speak to you when your house is in order.

When I read the words "obviously you cannot transmit something you haven't got," I shuddered at the fact that I could no longer hide or con my way through life. Humility was the first clear example of what this meant for me. I learned through study that humility cannot be purchased, read about, or given away. Humility must be experienced in order for someone to become a humble person. Enduring adversity builds charac-ter and transmits humility.

This is the Great Fact. This is also known as the Great Commission. Leave your doubt and unbelief behind, and go and make more of you. Carry this message!

STUDY EXCERPT: "Abandon yourself to God as you understand God. Admit your faults to Him and to your fellows. Clear away the wreckage of your past. Give freely of what you find and join us. We shall be with you in the Fellowship of the Spirit, and you will surely meet some of us as you trudge the Road of Happy Destiny. May God bless you and keep you—until then."

When I read the word "trudge," I thought to myself, "What a word!" I had to look it up to get a clear meaning of it. Trudge has synonyms like "plod," "labor," "drag," and "struggle." Life certainly has events that seem to fit with the word "trudge." It was never said that life would be a skip-pitty-do-da-day every day! But, when the peace of a day can outlast the challenges of life, what a wonderful day it is!

Again, exercise your enthusiasm to learn and look up these scripture verses and apply them.

RELIANCE: Synonyms are "dependence," "confidence," and "trust."
Psalm 125:2
Ezekiel 36:27
Isaiah 52:12

FELLOWSHIP: Synonyms are "association," "companionship," and "group."
1 Corinthians 1:10
Galatians 6:2, 10
Romans 12:9–10
Philippians 1:3, 27

CRAVE: Synonyms are "to desire," "to hunger after," and "to ask humbly for."
Matthew 5:6
Psalm 37:4

FACT: Synonyms are "reality," "truth," and "information."
Proverbs 10:9, 31
Colossians 3:9
Ephesians 4:25
Romans 8:26

Chapter Six

STUDY OF

"SERENITY PRAYER"

Serenity Prayer: God grant me the serenity to accept the things I cannot change; the courage to change the things I can and the wisdom to know the difference. Living one day at a time, enjoying one moment at a time; Accepting hardship as a pathway to peace; Taking, as Jesus did this sinful world as it is, Not as I would have it; Trusting that You will make all things right if I surrender to Your will; So that I may be reasonably happy in this life and supremely happy with You forever in the next. Amen.

REINHOLD NIEBUHR

The Serenity Prayer is actually a problem-solving tool. Let us take a look at the deeper meaning of key words in this prayer.

STUDY EXCERPT: "God grant me the serenity…"

Grant: Synonyms include "to award," "to present," "to bestow," and there are many more. So why should God grant us something unless something has changed? Is it action along with the Twelve Steps that creates some quality that should be rewarded? At the Third Step where we turn our lives and our wills over to the care of God, surely this is the change that needs to take place (just for starters). For this, God will *grant* us rewards.

Serenity: Synonyms are "tranquil," "calmness," and "contentment."

Serenity means more than happiness, peace, and contentment. It is immeasurable. It is more than more. It keeps growing as we grow spiritually. Serenity is above understanding, and it is real! "Thou wilt keep him in perfect peace, whose mind is stayed on thee: because he trusteth in thee" (Isaiah 26:3, KJV). "Peace I leave with you, my peace I give unto you: not as the world giveth, give I unto you. Let not your heart be troubled, neither let it be afraid" (John 14:27, KJV). "Those things, which ye have both learned, and received, and heard, and seen in me, do: and the God of peace shall be with you" (Philippians 4:9, KJV).

STUDY EXCERPT: "...to accept the things I cannot change..."

Accept: Synonyms are "to agree to," "to recognize," and "to understand." So I ask God to grant me acceptance.

Change: Synonyms are "to transform," "to revolutionize," and "to alter." I accept those things I cannot change about anyone else (people, circumstances, etc.) and put them into my prayers. Yes, Let go and let God! Nothing happens in God's world by mistake. "Cannot change" refers to the fact that *of our own power* we cannot change those things. "Call unto me, and I will answer thee, and show thee great and mighty things, which thou knowest not" (Jeremiah 33:3, KJV). "For my thoughts are not your thoughts, neither are your ways my ways, saith the Lord" (Isaiah 55:8, KJV).

Things: Synonyms are "possessions," "happenings," and "details." The word "things" is all-inclusive; it leaves nothing out. Everything that exists falls under the word "thing." "And we know that all things work together for good to them that love God, to them who are the called according to his purpose" (Romans 8:28, KJV).

STUDY EXCERPT: "...the courage to change the things I can... "

Courage: Synonyms are "bravery," "guts," and "daring." So I ask God to grant me courage to change those things about myself (my attitudes, my knowledge, my way of thinking, etc.) that need changing. This is not about fear. Making changes is about determination in spite of any fear. We must become willing and we must rely on God for the strength. "That he would grant you, according to the riches of his glory, to be strengthened with might by his Spirit in the inner man" (Ephesians 3:16, KJV). "But they that wait upon the Lord shall renew their strength; they shall mount up with wings as eagles; they shall run, and not be weary; and they shall walk, and not faint" (Isaiah 40:31, KJV). "I can do all things through Christ which strengtheneth me" (Philippians 4:13, KJV).

STUDY EXCERPT: "...and the wisdom to know the difference."

Wisdom: Synonyms are "good judgment," "insight," and "good sense." Wisdom is the ability to discern the true from the false. Wisdom does not necessarily refer to book smarts or intelligence. Many of God's people have intelligence, but they can't make a good decision because they can't see what is right or wrong, what is good or evil. Wisdom may not come with age alone. You may have to pray for it. "How much better to get wisdom than gold! And to get understanding is to be chosen rather than silver" (Proverbs 16:16, NKJV). "Let your heart retain my words; Keep my commands, and live. Get wisdom! Get understanding! Do not forget, nor turn away from the words of my mouth. Do not forsake her, and she will preserve you; Love her, and she will keep you. Wisdom is the principal thing; Therefore get wisdom" (Proverbs 4:4–7, NKJV).

Know: Synonyms are "to identify," "to recognize," and "to understand." In order to know something you must have the facts (truth).

Difference: Synonyms are "distinction," "discrepancy," and "change." The word difference in this prayer simply means understanding when to accept the things we cannot change in others and to change those things we can in ourselves. You will have to make a choice between them, and good judgment is required!

STUDY EXCERPT: "Living One day at a time, enjoying one moment at a time…"

Living: Synonyms are "alive," "active," "existing." It is time to live. Knowing what you are saved for is the key to being alive and active, and not just existing.

Day: Synonyms are "day of the week," "time," and "date." I had no idea how long twenty-four hours was until I sobered up. It was a long, long time when I first sobered up. Now there are not enough hours in a day to get done everything that I want to do. "Give us this day our daily bread" (Matthew 6:11, NKJV). "Do not boast about tomorrow, for you do not know what a day may bring forth" (Proverbs 27:1, NKJV).

Enjoying: Synonyms are "to take pleasure in," "to like," and "to get pleasure from." Today I truly can say I enjoy each moment I have every day. At work I try to be the best employee, enjoying my achievements and a job well done. At home I truly enjoy every moment I have to spend with my husband and fellowship with others. There is so much pleasure in living a righteous life. The challenges are there, but so is the glory. "This is the day the Lord has made; we will rejoice and be glad in it" (Psalm 118:24, NKJV).

STUDY EXCERPT: "…Accepting hardship as a pathway to peace…"

Hardship: Synonyms are "suffering," "difficulty," and "adversity." "We are hard-pressed on every side, yet not crushed; we are perplexed, but not in despair; persecuted, but not forsaken; struck down, but not destroyed" (2 Corinthians 4:8–9, NKJV). "Though I walk in the midst of trouble, thou wilt revive me: thou shalt stretch forth thine hand against the wrath of mine enemies, and thy right hand shall save me" (Psalm 138:7, KJV).

Pathway: Synonyms are "way," "conduit," and "trail." The word "pathway" refers back to the opening sentence of "How It Works" so appropriately. "Rarely have we seen a person fail who has thoroughly followed our path."

Peace: Synonyms are "calm," "reconciliation," and "harmony." "Be careful for nothing; but in every thing by prayer and supplication with thanksgiving let your requests be made known unto God. And the peace of God, which passeth all understanding, shall keep your hearts and minds through Christ Jesus" (Philippians 4:6-7, KJV).

STUDY EXCERPT: "…Taking, as Jesus did, this sinful world as it is, not as I would have it…"

Taking: Synonyms are "winning," "captivation," and "attracting." "The Lord taketh pleasure in them that fear him, in those that hope in his mercy" (Psalm 147:11, KJV).

Sinful: Synonyms are "corrupt," "immoral," and "wicked." "For all have sinned and fall short of the glory of God" (Romans 3:23, NKJV). Those of us in addictions are confronted with our lawlessness as well as our character defects.

World: Synonyms are "mankind," "humanity," and "the human race." "For God so loved the world, that he gave his only begotten Son, that whosoever believeth in him should not perish, but have everlasting life" (John 3:16, KJV).

STUDY EXCERPT: "…Trusting that You will make all things right if I surrender to Your will…"

Trusting: Synonyms are "to hope," "to have faith in," and "to depend on." "And be found in him, not having mine own righteousness, which is of the law, but that which is through the faith of Christ, the righteousness which is of God by faith" (Philippians 3:9, KJV). Our doubt and unbelief have got to go. This is the turning point where we must trust Him with complete abandon.

Right: Synonyms are "correct," "appropriate," and "just." "For with the heart man believeth unto righteousness; and with the mouth confession is made unto salvation" (Romans 10:10, KJV). "And if Christ be in you, the body is dead because of sin; but the Spirit is life because of righteousness" (Romans 8:10, KJV).

Surrender: Synonyms are "to give in," "to relinquish," and "to submit." Here at Step Three we must surrender to His will or remain in rebellion. Without God there is no hope for real happiness.

STUDY EXCERPT: "...So that I may be reasonably happy in this life and supremely happy with You forever in the next."

Reasonably: Synonyms are "sensibly," "logically," and "realistically." Did we ever do anything reasonably? We wanted more of everything and gave less of ourselves for it.

Happy: Synonyms are "contented," "joyfully," and "pleased." To be happy with ourselves and show a little joy by a smile on our faces is the beginning of a new life for us.

Supremely: Synonyms are "completely," "absolutely," and "totally." The word "supremely" was a new word for my vocabulary. I know today that I want more of Him and less of everything else. I want to be supremely happy with Him forever!

Forever: Synonyms are "evermore," "ceaselessly," and "without end." "Verily, verily, I say unto you, He that believeth on me hath everlasting life" (John 6:47, KJV). "Surely goodness and mercy shall follow me all the days of my life: and I will dwell in the house of the Lord forever" (Psalm 23:6, KJV).

Prayer is not a weapon, or even a part of the armor that we dress in. Prayer is the means by which we engage in the battle itself, and it is the purpose for which we get armed. To put on the armor of God is to prepare for battle. Prayer is the battle itself, with God's Word being our chief weapon. I still fight today, only my weapons are different! Please read this over several times before going on.

Chapter Seven

TESTIMONIES

PATT

I am a believer who struggled with codependency and alcohol. The first time I was exposed to the Twelve Steps it was in Alcoholics Anonymous, and they gave me sobriety from alcohol. I was on the Fourth Step working this program when my sponsor sent me to Adult Children of Alcoholics (ACA), and Codependents Anonymous (Coda) to find myself and identify where the pain in my life was coming from. In other words, my sponsor recognized her limitations, and I recognized her frustrations in working with me. The last thing my sponsor told me to do was to go to my chemically dependent meetings daily. So, I went to three or four or more meetings every day. I started with one A.A. meeting a day plus whatever other Twelve Step meeting was on the schedule. I am still grateful to this day for what I learned about myself in all Twelve Step arenas, because, no matter what the addiction was that was being addressed, the Twelve Step Programs all used the same basic process. My first lesson was that it was not my sponsor's responsibility to fix me, but my responsibility to make my recovery happen despite my attitude. Then Mercy walked into my life. Yes, God's mercy (God's ability to hold from me what I deserve) and grace (God's ability to give me what I don't deserve).

Those sharing their experience, strength, and hope in Coda meetings gave me a sense of choice about my recovery from the pain identified in codependency. I looked for the easier, softer way and could not find it. I prayed for it, waited for it, searched for it, longed for it, and hoped for the key that would unlock this mystery of recovery in my life. I can't count how many times I attended seminars, bought books, and went to counseling hoping to be transformed and relieved of this pain I carried. I came to know that the Twelve Steps are the core for transformation and the path to recovery. The old-timers would say, "You can dance around these steps all you want and suit up and sit in meetings forever. But when you choose to change your life, you will begin to work these steps." Every book, seminar, and counseling session enhanced my recovery when I started working these steps.

At Twelve Step meetings, the group would read what was called the Promises. At the end of the Promises we read the statement, "God will do for us what we cannot do for ourselves." How profound those words were. Later the revelation would kick in! I sat in my meetings for so long, focusing on my problems of caretaking, shame, controlling, obsessing, victimization, and self-loathing (for starters), instead of focusing on the solution. Putting down the alcohol giant and prescription drug giant was nothing compared to this giant called codependency. These Steps changed me and transformed me in ways that I had to experience and not just intellectualize. I was told in meetings many times that in order to become a humble person, one must experience humility!

It is with the greatest respect for the Twelve Steps that I share this part of my journey, where I found myself and my purpose in life. Working the steps meant making an effort to apply principles to my life, and when I did, what a profound behavioral, emotional, and spiritual result occurred. A significant personality change took place in my very being! I no longer talked the same, walked the same, or went to the same places. One example was that after a few months of sobering up, a coworker came up to me and asked me if I was on drugs. "Wow," I thought to myself. "Have I changed that much?"

Immediately, Step One gave me permission to stop controlling, deal with my fear, and take care of myself at work. But, I found myself trying to control others, namely my children and family, well into my recovery process. I had driven off a husband and all my close friends, except my one childhood friend Carol. She listened to my whining and crying and is still my pal.

Although it may be subdued today, that sinful controlling nature can rear its head at any given moment. I had made myself feel crazy, and my life had become unmanageable with both overt and subtler attempts to control many people. I was trying to control what they did, thought, felt, and how and when they changed. I had been too enmeshed with the life of my children and out of touch with myself. I was caught in a torrent of obsessive thinking—not saying no, not saying what I meant, not being in touch with what I wanted and needed, not having boundaries, and not living my own life. These patterns are what created this giant of codependent unmanageability. When I look at the pattern of my life, I can identify this generational sickness.

I didn't start drinking until I was twenty years old. Fear kept me from what I hated the most, which was *out of control* people. When I was a child I used to put my shoes by the bed at night just in case I had to run. I was always trying to run and hide. I would go out the door by the kitchen, grab a coat, and run out to the garage. If I couldn't get out unnoticed, I went and hid in the bedroom closet. I would crawl into the very back and hide under whatever I could stack on top of me.

There were many incidents related to my parents' toxic behavior that I reacted to, and this abuse took many forms: emotional and physical abandonment, neglect, verbal abuse, physical abuse, alcoholism, and more. One night that I remember in particular, I really believed my father was going to kill my mother. My father had come home from work drunk, like many times before, but that particular night my mother would not stop yelling. She always tried to control by yelling back, which made my father react, and then the hell would start. My little brother, who was six years younger than me, happened to be at home with me that night. My older sister and brother were always gone, staying at other people's homes. The next thing I knew, my brother and I wanted to escape, but we couldn't get out of the house. So we went upstairs to the attic bedroom. I was sitting at the top of the stairs, shaking uncontrollably. I was no longer aware of anything but my shaking. Then it was morning, and I came down the stairs. It was a natural reaction to just start cleaning up the mess of broken furniture and blood in the kitchen and bathroom. To my amazement, I noticed that not a single window was broken. At least people driving by wouldn't notice what had happened again. The family secrets were still protected.

My father died at the age of forty-four, when I was twenty years old, and at that time the family was uncontrollable. So I bought a one-way ticket to Cincinnati, Ohio, where my maternal grandparents lived. You could say I ran away from home when I was twenty-one. Later a psychologist told me healthy children run away at twelve. I had no intentions of going back home to Washington, so I got a job and lived with my aunt and uncle until my drinking had escalated and I was sinking in sin. I was teaching Sunday school classes and drinking with the whole family on a regular basis!

Sin is what separated me from everything I longed for. By age twenty-four, I was an unwed mother. Oh, what shame I brought upon this Irish Catholic family. My feelings were that I didn't need these people anyway. Now, with my baby, I would have someone who really loved me. I sued my child's father for $25.00 a week to cover childcare, so I could continue working and take care of myself. I didn't need anyone.

My mother remarried and soon asked if my little brother could come and live with me. He had been getting in trouble, and according to my mother it was our cousin's fault (not the fault of my brother's addictions). He came to live with me, and I bought an old car for him to get to and from a vocational school. Soon the school called and wanted to know why he wasn't coming. He was an out of control drug addict. Every day was a nightmare. I found myself packing the baby's diaper bag and putting my shoes and purse by the back door of my trailer—just in case I had to run. The night came when that giant went on a rampage. The police were called, and it took four of them to put my brother on a straight board and shackle him. He was bleeding from tearing up the house with his fists, so he was taken to the hospital. In the hospital he was left on the straight board shackled, yelling that he was going to kill me if I didn't get him out of there. After seven hours he came down off of what ever he was on, and we left the hospital as if nothing happened. He just walked out after they unshackled him.

After a few days I escorted him back to Washington State via an airplane. I had not been home for six years. That very night after the family gathering, my brother came home from wherever he had been drugging and started fighting with my mother. She tried to control him just like she had my father. I was in the back bedroom with my baby, shaking uncontrollably. I kept saying to myself, "I will be on a plane in two days, and I am never coming back." This was the same house, thirteen years after the incident with my parents, only six years after my father's death, and I was experiencing alcohol and drug addiction of the next generation.

By twenty-six, I married a man I did not love. I had no real concept of love at that time. The only thing I was sure of was that he would not hit me. I had known him since I was six years old. Our fathers worked together and drank together. My decisions were made with logic or lust, or both. Now I had a drinking partner, and we had two more children. We drank drink for drink, and it would behoove him to be sure I had all I needed.

When I reached the saturation level of alcohol, it caused ugly depressions, and then I would go to the psychiatrist and switch to Valium. The family much preferred me going to shrinks and on prescriptions. I never thought about whether I was actually getting better or worse; I just went back to the doctor, and he changed the color of my Valium. I just took it. I did not want to feel. My prescription drugs were still keeping me from dealing with me. That cycle went on for the eight years I was married to my now ex-husband.

Finally, I stopped the Valium and started losing weight and thinking more about my career. I was always thinking about *my* and *I*. When I went to the doctor, he was very surprised to see how healthy I looked, and he asked me if I was getting a divorce. All he did was plant a thought in my head. That thought said, "Why not?" I filed for a divorce, and for the next two years my ex-husband and I fought for control of the children and possessions. We also had to go in front of a judge over the children's visitation and financial support before the divorce was over.

The judge said, "I can't tell which one of you is lying," and she asked if we wanted a guardian ad litem. In total ignorance, I said, "Yes." Now I really had to protect the lies and the secrets about my drinking. Needless to say, the three-story home with a water view, the Dalmatian dog in the window, the van and matching car were all lost due to the fight for control. At the end of the divorce, after fighting for two straight years, the kids were left, and nothing else survived.

Now the children were taking care of themselves. We went through an additional five years of custody battles after the divorce. My ex-husband married a woman who had practiced witchcraft in the past. The children were exposed to ouija boards, ghosts living in the house, and astrology readings when visiting. Even living the out of control and godless life that I was, I had to get the children out of my ex-husband's house. So I put in for a promotion to Yuma, Arizona. It took the judge and guardian ad litem to get me out of Washington with my children. But I was still thinking only of *I* and *my*.

Through God's mercy and grace, I sobered up eight months later in Yuma. But now I found myself putting my shoes and purse by the window just in case I had to run because of the fear of my children. All three children were using and drinking and questioning me, saying, "Who do you think you are to tell us what to do?" My sponsor told me to leave those kids alone. I would face that giant soon enough. All three of my children had alcohol and drug addictions. This was the next generation. Runaway children were living in and on top of my house.

The day I faced this next-generation giant, I called on God in the spiritual realm and the police in the natural. I announced to my kids in the presence of the police that if what they were doing was against the law it was not negotiable and I would turn them in to the law. This was now tough love. So I told them it would be a good idea to tell their friends that I was not turning them in; I was only turning my children in to the law.

On that day, I identified where my pain was coming from. The wounded children I saw standing in my home overwhelmed me. I knew that I was now well-equipped with the Twelve Steps to change myself and to give this gift of living to my children. As a survivor, I wanted so much to stop this legacy of abuse and abandonment. I had become aware of how the abusive behaviors of my parents drove my life. And I was now aware of how I had repeated that abusive behavior with my children. I announced that we were going to go as a family to church or my Twelve Step Program. I left it up to them, and of course they chose the Twelve Step Program. Church was never a part of their lives, and they did not know that I had met Jesus in my Twelve Step Program. An old-timer had given to me the book *The Sermon on the Mount* by Emmet Fox. The co-founders of the Twelve Steps used the Bible, *The Sermon on the Mount,* and a leaflet called the *Upper Room* before they divinely put together their program. I had studied the history of the Twelve Steps and found this out in my search for the truth. I now knew the truth about Jesus and my relationship with him.

For the next three years, the roller coaster ride was constant. My older son quit school. My second son was getting into gang activity. My daughter was just a mess and violently rebellious. During the next three years, tough love would prevail. I put my older son out of the house because he chose not to return to school or get a job. Then he found a job and left for Idaho with a contractor. I told him to call home collect anytime he wanted as well as confirming that I loved him.

I then had to seek help for my second son. He was out of control, and Juvenile Authorities told me to let him stay with someone else so that I would not get hurt. I went to the treatment center and made arrangements to get him in there. Juvenile was notified of the arrangements and sent the police with me to get my son from his friend's home. My second son was in treatment for thirty days. I rested knowing that he was safe. I went to the treatment center three times a week for one-on-one family counseling and multi-family counseling. After thirty days he came home, and the very next day my daughter was arrested outside of the house for domestic violence. I went back to the same treatment center and they gave me a package deal. She entered treatment and was there for three months.

The family and ex-family all were convinced I was the only problem.

My children's father was supposed to carry medical insurance on them, and he did. But after the treatment was over, we found out it did not cover them out of the state of Washington. I was financially bankrupt. Once these two younger kids were out of treatment, they were put in special education. Next thing I knew, my older son called, wanting to come home. I could not deal with all of this so I called my little brother, who had sat on the top of those stairs with me way back when, and asked him to take my son into his home and put him back in school.

Several years before, my little brother had been committed to Western State Hospital and put on the criminally insane ward for a three-year sentence. He spent his twenty-first birthday in that mental hospital. All of this was a result of drugs and alcohol. One little old lady came to the Twelve Step meetings in that ward every Thursday evening for three years and told my brother that God saved him for something very special.

My brother took my older son in and put him back in school. God had saved my brother from drugs and alcohol for something very special; he was able to make amends to me and help my son. Two years passed, and my older son came home after he graduated from high school to see me before he went into the Army. It was a gift to see him.

I made an appointment for all of us to have our picture taken as a family. I knew it might be the last time I ever had the three of my kids together. We were getting ready to go, and the three of them were fighting over what clothes they were going to wear. They all came out with black on. I did not care. Then my older son went back in the room and put a purple shirt on over his black shirt. After the picture was taken, my older son left with his old friends from school, and my second son said he was going to a party. That was not allowed on intensive probation. I said, "I am not fighting with you anymore," so everybody left and I walked to a meeting. I was gone for a total of four hours, during which time some Marines picked up my second son off someone's yard and brought him home.

When I got home, I heard my son calling from the bathroom and pushed the door open. He had overdosed. The right side of his body was paralyzed, as if he had had a stroke. The ambulance was called, and the emergency room doctor, who was in my Twelve Step group, assured me he would let me know everything right away. My son had overdosed on straight Jack Daniels alcohol!

The next day, my older son left for the Army. Once he was out of basic training, he sent me a gift. The gift had a ceremonial letter that I was to read before I opened the small box. The letter said that what I was receiving was a medal of honor for being his mother. The letter went on about how I had held his hand when he was a baby, as he learned to walk. Then I had to let go of his hand. At the end of the letter it said he knew by high school that I wondered if my son was going to make it! I opened the box while tears flooded out of my eyes. The gift was a gold necklace with a diamond in the center. Receiving my medal of honor for being his mother was an experience of the Grace of God.

My son spent the next three years in Kuwait, Somalia, and another goodwill campaign. Then he settled in Virginia after he got out of the Army. My daughter now had a baby. The father was in jail, then more jail, then prison as a result of drugs and alcohol. When my older son heard the father was getting out of prison, he sent for his sister and her baby to start a new life back in Virginia. She left and spent three days on a bus to get there. She arrived in Virginia on Thanksgiving Day, and she spent the whole day with her brother. The very next morning my older son was shot and killed in a hunting incident. Our world was fractured.

I had spent a few years working on forgiveness while doing my steps. I went to the grief recovery institute and learned about forgiveness. Everything I knew and learned about forgiveness was slamming me in the face. The family was in a rage, and all I could do was stay focused on Jesus. I did not want to start questioning God. I felt so much gratitude for having sobered up in time to make those things right that I knew were seriously wrong. I worked the Twelve Steps. I made my amends to my children. Everything was right between my oldest son and me. Thank you, Jesus! My oldest son had given me back my dignity as a parent. My God, how I hung onto that. When I went to my son's funeral, I knew I would have to see this man who killed him and forgive him in order to keep my sanity and my sobriety.

After the funeral, the captain of the National Guard Unit where my son was a member made that man come to the Armory to face me. The man was the weapons safety officer for that guard unit. I remember looking into his glassy eyes, and when I reached to put my hand on his arm he pulled away. I told him that I forgave him but it didn't mean that I would not hold him accountable. I expected him to pay for the funeral and encouraged him to get to his pastor and find some peace. All he could do was to stand there frozen, and I felt so free of him. As I got back into the truck, the young man from the unit who took me home said, "That's the bravest thing I have ever seen." This young man was a sergeant in the United States Army, and this was the bravest thing he had seen. I had no anger or rage. It was over, because I obeyed God. "I can do all things through Christ which strengtheneth me" (Philippians 4:13, KJV). Now I could get back to my home in Arizona and begin healing and reaching out to my family.

"There are no answers." I repeated that statement to anyone who asked me questions, and went back to focusing on God's mercy and grace while going to meetings. Only God knows what happened out there in the woods when my son was shot, and I held onto that truth. There was only one witness as to where my son was standing originally. Thirty days after my son's death, that witness shot and killed himself the night before the first hearing. Again, there were no answers. Hearings went on for three years before it went to a jury trial. Then the jury let the man who killed my son off in the natural, but he was not let off in the spiritual! God only knows what happened.

There is an ongoing need for me to surrender and trust God as I walk this journey called recovery, and there is hope for recovery from a lifetime of unhealthy relationships *one day at a time*. Psalm 139:13–16 revealed to me that God saw me when I was in my mother's womb. He knew my mother and father and the circumstances of the home where I was to grow up. He knew the many schools I would attend and the neighborhoods in which I would live. God gave me the ability to develop survival techniques and walked with me through the good times and bad times. He gave the survival techniques and guardian angels to keep and protect me revealed in Psalm 91:11. He chose me before the foundation of the world to be holy and without blame before Him in love, as revealed in Ephesians 1:4.

He cried with me when I cried. He laughed when I laughed. He was grieved when I was abused. He watched and waited for me. He was looking to that day when I would repent of my ways and then receive Jesus as my Savior, as he waits for everyone. I know He longs for my asking, knocking, and seeking Him more and more intimately.

Your survival techniques were probably different than mine. Whatever they were, and whatever your life may have been like up to this point, I personally know that the peace of God can change the regrets and heal the wounds of the past, turning them into thanksgiving and praise. Life is exciting, and I am grateful that I am alive for such a time as this. I am an over-comer by the blood of the Lamb and by the word of my testimony.

FRITZI

Hello, my name is Fritzi. I am a believer who struggled with alcohol, illegal drugs, and prescription drugs. I grew up in a loving family with two brothers and a sister. The most important gift our parents gave us was the introduction to God. I accepted Jesus as my personal savior at about thirteen years old and lived a victorious Christian life until I was seventeen years old.

Then one short weekend, I took my eyes off of Jesus, which brought me thirty-plus years of emotional pain, physical trauma, and sadness. I met and married an unbeliever who introduced me to drugs and alcohol. Never did I imagine the pain and destruction that was in store for me, as well as for my children. After nine years of struggling in a marriage that inevitably was going from bad to worse, I filed for a divorce. The divorce was messy. I was hateful with only one goal in mind, which was getting even at any cost. Finally, after two years of fighting in and out of court, the divorce was final—on paper only. It was then I began using drugs and alcohol to anesthetize my pain and sadness, which started me on a downward spiral into my addictions.

Moving on to the next chapter in my life, I met and married yet another unbeliever. Now I found myself going deeper into the abyss of insanity with drugs and alcohol. I had surrounded myself with every kind of friend that could provide or join me in my addictions and sinful life. I thought the drugs were hidden from my children. I was displaying only the alcohol, because it was, at least, a legal drug. I was delusional and in denial, but my children knew the truth of it all. I was filled with guilt and shame and felt lost in the lifestyle I had chosen. My entitlement to do whatever I wanted became a monster. I would not look at what part I played in this destructive lifestyle. I felt like it was always someone else's fault. I made several attempts to stop, but that became futile. It all became a vicious circle!

I gathered as much emotional support as I possibly could every day from my drinking and drugging support groups, without actually taking the steps to quit. I had contact with my parents and my children, who would rather have a substance-abusing mother than no mother at all. I had created in my sick mind a false win-win situation with manipulation and lies.

With another alcohol-and-drug-based marriage approaching eight years now in dire straights, the craziness had come full circle. I was emotionally spent and feeling like a failure. I was convinced that my children would be better off with their father. With that thought in my head, I climbed into my vehicle prepared to go and tell the children's father he could have custody. It just so happens that the children were conveniently at their father's house for spring break.

Then suddenly, while I was driving down Highway 18, the lines dividing the road disappeared, leaving only one lane. I had enough presence of mind left to pull over to the side of the road, where I was found and taken to the hospital, having a nervous breakdown. Later I was released only to be put on anti-depressants to try and stabilize my mind. I acknowledged the need to make a change, but in my depression it seemed nearly impossible to think about change.

While my children were still at their father's house for spring break, I felt this might be a good time to try and take control of my life and try to work things out with my second husband. I got up the next morning and fixed his lunch to get him off to work. When he walked out the front door he noticed a gift box in the front seat of my vehicle.

I asked him to hand me the box, and then I sat it down at my antique sewing machine just inside the front door. The box was about the size of a corsage box. A card was glued to the top of the box that said, "Fritzi, especially for you." Just looking at the box, I was not suspicious, because friends had been very attentive with gifts and cards through this difficult time of my nervous breakdown. I did, however, wonder why it had a rubber band around it!

Upon removing the rubber band, the noise became deafening and the air turned black. The box contained a highly explosive pipe bomb. It blew me across my living room to the farthest exterior wall, which stopped me. I picked myself up off the floor, feeling a stinging sensation and a warmth all over my body. The stinging was gunpowder and shrapnel burning through the layers of my skin. The warmth was my own blood covering my body. My eardrums were fractured from the percussion, I had severe flash burn in my eyes, and my carotid artery had a piece of metal embedded in it. There was a hole through my left thigh where the bomb entered the front and exited the back of my leg. There were numerous injuries to my fingers and my overall body.

I was transported to Overlake Hospital. It seemed like time was standing still. After several weeks in the hospital and five surgeries performed by wonderful surgeons guided by God's hand, I was able to go home.

By this time my first husband, the father of my children, was now incarcerated for attempted murder in the first degree plus a charge for bombing. My second husband and I tried to put our marriage together, but to no avail, and we divorced less than a year after the bombing assault.

After more failed relationships, moving around to different locations, I decided to move back to the town I grew up in and be close to my family. I was still living in sin, and this, accompanied by my addictions, made my hometown yet another place to continue the insanity. I began living a nocturnal life with isolated tears.

By then, my children were following in my footsteps. I tried to get a handle on them, but I didn't have a handle on myself. Who was I kidding? As time went on, my son became more and more unmanageable. He was into drugs and alcohol full time, moving from one house to another. He was in and out of jail, finally going to prison for a full year.

Now my guilt was holding me hostage. I knew God should be the center of our lives, but I had ignored Him for so long. My children were paying the price for this along with me. With my self-respect at a complete minimum and my children at great risk, the pain finally outweighed the pleasure and I knew it was time for me to make a real change.

My boyfriend that I had been with for almost eight years at that time started noticing a difference in my personality. I was not enjoying going out anymore. Drugs and alcohol were at a minimum in my life. I was restless, agitated, and under conviction. One night a family member was visiting from out of town and wanted us to go out, so we all went to a local bar. As the night progressed, something happened to me that I will never forget. It was just after midnight. In the midst of the noise in that bar where we had gone, Jesus came to me. He said to me, "I love you. I am going to silence this place only to you, and I want you to see yourself in each person here and ask yourself if this is worth eternal life!" I began to look around, seeing myself in each person there in the bar. With tears streaming down my cheeks, I told my boyfriend I had to go home.

This was a Saturday night, and I knew I had a divine appointment with Jesus the next morning in church. Getting up and going to church was a hard thing for me to do. Why? Because I was taunted with the thought of how selfish I was to even consider purchasing eternal life through Jesus Christ when my children were unsaved. The mental fight had begun. Fighting for emotional sobriety, I pressed forward, and drove past the church at least three times. Finally, I parked my car and went in the church. Then I sat down in the most inconspicuous place, thinking I could slip out if I changed my mind.

Between Pastor Jennings preaching and Jesus tugging at my heart, I could not tell you what the sermon was about, but it had my attention. I was still trying to be invisible, but tears were running down my cheeks. Suddenly, I felt an arm around me. It was a friend I had grown up with in church, and her words to me were, "You do not have to hide anymore." I had now made up my mind and was waiting impatiently for the inevitable altar call.

The invitation was finally given to come forward. My eyes were burning from salty tears, and my heart was racing as I asked myself, "Do I dare take this step and risk a failed attempt?" The hardest part of that walk was stepping out from the pew, and from that point on there was only one set of footsteps as Jesus carried me the rest of the way. As my family stepped out to be with me it was like coming home again after a long, long journey. There is a verse in the book of James that says, "Humble yourselves in the sight of the Lord, and He will lift you up" (James 4:10, NKJV). And He did!

I left church that day knowing I had a lot of the unknown ahead of me. The difference now was that I was not walking alone. "Peace I leave with you, my peace I give unto you; not as the world giveth, give I unto you.

Let not your heart be troubled, neither let it be afraid" (John 14:27, KJV).

I did not know where to begin, so I just put everything in God's hands. I knew it would not be easy getting through all the baggage in my life. All I knew was that I had turned from a physical dependency to a spiritual dependency. The many remaining scars I had, both physical and emotional, served as reminders of what I was saved from. "He healeth the broken in heart, and bindeth up their wounds" (Psalm 147:3, KJV).

I went home and told my boyfriend Bill, whom I had lived with for eight years, what had happened. He said that was good and that he was glad. I was thinking, "Okay! What does that mean, and does he not know things are going to change a lot around here?" About three months went by, and a lot happened. Temptation to sin was fighting diligently to get me back. I was rebuking the thoughts of temptations on a continual basis. I moved forward in the Lord.

I soon came to a monumental crossroad. I was feeling convicted about living with Bill and not being married. I was even questioning if he was even the man God wanted me to be with. So I put it before God and said, "Your will be done, not mine." Then one night, sitting in the living room, I blurted out, "I cannot continue living with you without being married." He replied, "Okay, let's get married. I've asked you several times, you are the one that always said no." Nothing else was said for a few months.

Then one Sunday at church, we had a guest speaker by the name of Dr. Crouter. He had been to our church countless times. As I sat in the pew, Dr. Crouter looked into the congregation and said, "Now I am going to talk to you about some things that God is not pleased with in the church." He went on to say, "I have had people talk to me about living together, and they just don't know what to do, because they love each other but are not ready for marriage. Well, as an ambassador of Jesus Christ I have been given the authority to tell you to get married!" Feeling as though I was the only person sitting in the sanctuary with a target on my forehead, I knew what the conversation at our house would be that day when I got home. Again I said, "Bill, we need to get married." He said, "Okay." We were married within a month.

I then asked God, "Where do you want me, and what do you want me to do?" He said to my heart, "Look around you. Your mission field is all around you." So then I began volunteering in a recovery ministry. By 2006, my church started the Celebrate Recovery Twelve Step Fellowship, and I found my calling in leadership working with the chemically dependent group. I began a journey of a much deeper level than I had anticipated. Another woman, Patt, with twenty years of sobriety, was called to work in this same program because of her experience, strength, and hope in working the other Twelve Step Programs. She came up to me one evening as I was signing in for the meeting and asked me (with only three years of sobriety at the time) to be her sponsor. As I caught my breath, I reciprocated by asking her to be my sponsor. Patt said, "What came first, the chicken or the egg? I need a sponsor, too! The length of sobriety has nothing to do with the need for a sponsor."

As we began to meet, I did not really understand that I would literally have to work these steps. But gracious as she was, Patt began directing me in the process. She said to me, "If you don't work through these steps, how can you guide someone else through them?" She knew the pain I would experience. I wanted what she had, so I took that step of faith and did what she told me to do. Patt took me on a journey from admitting, to surrendering, to confessing, to repenting, to forgiving, and to service. I was astounded by the significant change that took place in me and my attitude about life and living.

In the fall of 2007, Patt suggested we have a retreat for our newly founded group of women in recovery. We could go out to her sister's cabin on Wildberry Lake in Mason County. Patt had an agenda to take us on a spiritual journey that none of us could have imagined. Eight women showed up for the weekend out of the ten to twelve who came regularly to our weekly meeting. The fellowship was glorious, and on Friday night we arrived at the cabin one after the other, having followed directions by watching for paper plates attached to trees along the road. We had a camp fire, ate, and laughed as Patt warned us to get our flashlights out before it got dark. She did not give us any electricity from the generator. This was a time that she made us withdraw from the world. Truly we were all affected by the withdrawal of all conveniences. A time to communicate was at hand. After we all got snuggled in bed and quit laughing, the silence was deafening. Patt slept on the couch downstairs next to the wood burning stove and kept the fire going all night.

Saturday morning arrived as we were awakened at 7:00 A.M. by an alarm of praise and worship music. Pancakes were cooking on the stove, eggs were frying, and the smell of coffee was in the air. Everyone began to stir out of bed. By 9:00 A.M. we were all settled down on the couches and ready to spend the morning and afternoon with Juanita Bynum's video conference called *Behind the Veil*. It truly stretched us all. The Spirit of the Lord ascended over us, and our unity was solidified. I cannot put in words what I saw in our group as we began to ascend spiritually to a new level. I have been behind that veil more than once since that weekend. Now all I want is more of Jesus!

Every woman at that retreat weekend had a sponsor and was working the steps. In the beginning Patt and I were the two sponsors who had thoroughly worked these steps. I encourage you now to get a sponsor and work these steps if you have not already done so. Keep working with that sponsor, because she needs you as much as you need her! And that is all I am going to say about that. Easy does it, but do it!

Joe Stowell, author of devotional books such as *Simply Jesus and You*, revealed to me how we are a fallen race planted in a fallen place. The Bible will keep you from sin, or sin will keep you from the Bible. Standing before you today, I am a miracle of His mercy and grace. I was given a second chance to stand before God with the promise of eternal life. I am forgiven. I prayed many times, saying, "Oh God, please change this circumstance," only to have God reveal to me that He may not change the circumstance, but He will change me in the circumstance.

I would like to share a scripture that tells my story: "I waited patiently for the Lord; and inclined unto me, and heard my cry. He brought me up also out of a horrible pit, out of the miry clay, and set my feet upon a rock, and established my goings" (Psalm 40:1-2, KJV).

People have their own ideas of addiction. Clearly an addiction can be anything you won't give up. If your children's faces look worried and sad, if tears fill the eyes of your parent, if people who used to look at you with pride now look away from you with shame, if family and friends will not let their children visit you, if your husband or wife sits in a chair looking for your car to pull in, if there is a muffled sobbing, if your bills are not getting paid, if you are losing the stability of life and you are more comfortable in darkness than in the light, you have an addiction. You have an addiction that is going to rob you of family, friends, financial security, and self-respect. But most important of all, it will rob you of your eternal life with Jesus.

However, because of redemption through Jesus, it does not have to be that way for you. If you take that first step, Jesus will take it from there. You have to be willing. "If ye shall ask any thing in my name, I will do it" (John 14:14, KJV). How much simpler can it be?

Remember that acceptance buys you a one-way ticket to eternity with Him. So today I ask you, "Should you take your last breath right now, where will you spend eternity?"

GLENDA

Hi, my name is Glenda, and I am a believer. I deal with codependency and overeating. I am a people pleaser. I would do just about anything others expected me to do to get my needs satisfied. This has complicated my life a great deal depending on whom I happen to be following at the time. My own life is put aside as I am too busy trying to please others. My actions are due to how I perceive what someone may think of me, rather than how I think of myself.

I came to codependent behaviors quite young. I attempted to protect my mother and brother from a raging father. Fear of my father's anger totally controlled me. I tried to solve my parents fighting and keep the family calm. One of the ways I did this was to hide my brother and keep him quiet. Trying to please my raging father was the next step, and by the time I was ready for school all my mental attention was focused on other people and relieving their pain. That made for a strange little girl who had a lot of problems. One problem I had was I could only eat corn. I only ate corn until I saw an allergy doctor.

School days of kindergarten were fun for me, and I became the Dear Abby of Mrs. Schroeder's class. I don't remember the problems, but I remember the kids. I always got into trouble for talking too much; one day I even got a spanking for it. One day in Miss Smith's first grade class I got a little friend to talk to and take home after class, and all my attention was on being a good friend to her. One day she got in a verbal fight with another little girl, and I backed up my friend, saying this other little girl was awful, etc. Then my friend made up with this little girl, but the little girl remembered what I said and I lost her friendship, such as it was. I remember how crushed I felt.

By the end of second grade my parents finally took me to see an allergy doctor, and I got an allergy test done. Many scratches later, they found out I was allergic to everything to eat but corn. So I started receiving allergy shots. By fourth grade I was starting to eat normally and got fat. That is when mom and dad started fighting about my weight, and I learned to control them a little bit by eating or not.

By the fifth and sixth grade I was very overweight. I ate and ate. I had one close friend by the name of Pam. All my good feelings about myself stemmed from that relationship. I lived in fear that I would do something that would make her mad at me. It was a good relationship for me, though, because Pam was pretty easygoing and our conflicts where few and did not amount to much. I did not bother with other friends. I just concentrated on Pam. I figured we would be friends forever. We joined Girl Scouts together and were in the same troop, we sold cookies together. We did everything together. Then one day came the crushing blow: she was moving to California. Her mother was getting a promotion at work. We vowed to write, and we did way into high school. She left the summer after sixth grade, and I finally stopped eating. I went the other way. I ate little or nothing at all.

That summer I became a butterfly. I went from a fat child to a thin woman. I looked sixteen, not twelve. I gained a new friend called Dee, who had a wealth of problems for me to try and solve. I started to notice boys, and they started to notice me. But my attitude toward others, I am sorry to say, was about what they could do for me. Except Dee, of course. My attitude with her was about what I could do for her. I did not think at all about God, if there was one or not. My dad said only weak people leaned on God, and my mom was a Baptist who never went to church. She had sent my brother Dewayne and me to church with her religious relatives once or twice. I learned that you were really quiet in church or people gave you really dirty looks. That's all I knew about Christians, except that they always wanted money, according to dad.

Seventh, eighth, and ninth grades were exciting. It was in junior high when I fell in love for the first time. Doug and I went steady the entire seventh through ninth grade. I was very codependent on him. All my good feelings came from being loved by him. I looked for his approval in everything I did. My entire dream for the future was linked to Doug. Doug went to a youth group at his church and introduced me to it, so I kind of was introduced to God. First I went just to be close to Doug, but I became interested myself. That summer, in summer school art class, I made a cross necklace and I never took it off. It was my sign that I had a relationship with Jesus. I didn't know what that meant, but it meant something to me. Unfortunately for me, Doug had a best friend who did not like me, by the name of Stu, and by ninth grade our relationship ended because of Stu. That is why I suffered a major nervous breakdown. I ended up in a state mental hospital for a year.

The year in the hospital was very painful; being a teenager in a locked down ward was very hard. I had actually enjoyed going to school. I excelled at school and got As. In the hospital they diagnosed me as schizophrenic, and it was a scary and lonely time for me. I gained weight while I was in the hospital during the first part of my stay. I ate well. I ate anything they would put in front of me. About the only thing I could control was my food. I learned through therapy two important things about myself:

1) that I loved God, and
2) that I loved my country.

The blackest points in my life were in that hospital, though some things that happened there were so bad that I have no memory of them. In February of 1970, I was released from the hospital and sent home to live again with my family, who enrolled me in the same high school I was in before the breakdown. That was a big mistake.

The kids teased me mercilessly. They had me coming and going with their comments about being crazy this and crazy that. So I turned to drugs and the occult. I got my friends to do séances to try to raise the dead. All we did was raise a lot of demons. I learned spells and chants. I got sicker and sicker.

I was terrible to people: my attitude was me first all the time. I was mean to my friend Dee. I would betray her and not think anything of it. I finally had a bad LSD trip and wound up in the hospital, and my dad came to get me. He yelled at me and lectured me. I did not go to school that day.

One day I got my dad real good and mad at me. I knew that he would really yell, and I was afraid of my dad, so I opted to go to the jail instead of calling him and going home with him. Dad came by that night, but I would not see him. That morning I went home, but not without the state noticing that I went to jail rather than going home. So a social worker came to see me, and I told her about my dad's temper and how everyone had to keep it a secret. He lost it all the time. The next thing I knew I was going to a group home in Ft. Wayne, Indiana. I was not eating again and had lost weight.

When I got to Ft. Wayne, I lived in an old house with fourteen girls in it, including me, a set of house parents, and one foster mother, Mrs. Lee. Mrs. Lee cared about us girls. She was Chinese, and she always got her English confused. For her the phrase "go jump in the lake" became "jump to the lake." She made us laugh. I went to school at the group home and graduated while I was there. A girl there by the name of Tina introduced me to a friend of her boyfriend's: Bruce.

Bruce went on to become my boyfriend of three years and my future husband. Of course I was codependent on him in all the typical ways. Needless to say it was not healthy, but on June 30, 1974, I married him, and Mrs. Lee had a reception at her house for us after the wedding. We fought before the marriage and fought double time afterwards. He liked to party and do drugs and would leave me at home sometimes for weeks on end before coming home again.

Then he wanted to have a son, and I agreed, so I got pregnant with my first child. January 6, 1975, Edward Steven was born. I thought that would change Bruce, but it did not. The first night home from the hospital he wanted to go party. He left us home alone just as much as before.

I left my husband the following April, and because I was a Bahai I began a one-year period of no dating called a year of patience. Bahais believe that all religions are right and they have different dispensations of the same thing. For instance, they believe that Jesus was a prophet, but not the Son of God. During the year of patience I was eating little to nothing. I got down to 115 pounds, which is not much weight for my frame.

My close friend came to my house, took me to my room, and removed my blouse. She put me in front of a mirror, and I could see my ribs. She said to me, "Are you anorexic?" I laughed it off and said no, but I knew I was not eating. I tried from then on to eat healthy. I mean, did I really have food problems? Me? Food occupied much of my time, and I did try to throw up after binging sometimes. I was preoccupied with being thinner, and I would starve to make up for my binge eating. Then there was the exercising and laxatives. Did I have a food problem? No, it had to be somebody else. I mean, my dad and Bruce had even said I was overweight. I soon gained ten pounds and forgot about eating problems.

In October of the year of patience I met a man by the name of Gordon. We began corresponding with each other long distance as he lived in Great Lakes, Illinois, and I was still in Indiana. He did fly in to see me on weekends, and this raised some eyebrows because we were not supposed to be dating, due to my year of patience. We continued to see each other the remainder of the year of patience that ended in April of 1976. My civil divorce ended in May, and Gordon asked me to marry him on the fourth of July, 1976. On August 17 of that year we had a Bahai wedding. I married a sailor, so off I went to Great Lakes.

The Great Lakes were interesting, and Gordon and I rented our own little house. He had his stuff already moved in by the time we got there. We picked up a bedroom set on the way to Great Lakes at a yard sale. I had a bed that I got from my family. We were given little things here and there and of course wedding presents. We were so happy. We made this house our home. We got together with the other Bahais, and our big goal was to become big enough to become a local assembly (which required nine people). We didn't have nine people yet, so we had to have firesides, which were meetings open to the public to find out about the Bahai faith. We opened our house up to have firesides.

I started to eat again but stayed at 125 pounds. I kept busy. I took care of Ed, the house, and took in extra kids to care for, for extra money. Time went by quickly, and a few years later, in 1979, Gordon and I had two sons of our own. Gordon had officially adopted Ed, so he was now a Bailey. About that time something happened that rattled our faith in the Bahais. We were introduced to Dixie, a woman who was a Christian and bound and determined to introduce us to Jesus. She asked me if I ever read the Bible. I said no, and she said, "Why not?" I couldn't give her an answer, because as Bahais we could read all religious writings. I started to read the New

Testament, because she told me to read the New Testament. I read it once, then twice. She asked me to go to a Bible study with her and asked me to meet with a student pastor. This went on for quite some time. I began to see that Bahai was not what it claimed to be. Some of its writings that were supposed to be new came from the Bible. Scripture from the Bible like "Jesus told him, 'I am the way, the truth, and the life. No one can come to the Father except through me'" (John 14:6, NLT), hit home. If Jesus was the only way, then how could we get there this other way? We couldn't! I began to think about these things.

Then one day at a Bible study in Dixie's home, Dixie said, "Glenda, you are going to hell if you don't accept Jesus." And I said, "Maybe I deserve to go to hell. I don't want to go to heaven just because of some fire insurance. Dixie, I want to love and know and serve Jesus with all my heart." And the minute I said it I knew it was true. April 24, at 11:00 A.M. Chicago time in 1981, I became a Christian and asked Jesus into my heart. I started to go to Church and ordered my first Bible. I had been reading a great big family Bible. It was the Living Bible and I read it until it fell apart. Also I began eating, and I weighed 180 pounds. I was no longer exercising or throwing up.

Gordon was not pleased that I had become a Christian. He was worried, especially since my church met in a high school and it was the days of the Jim Jones affair with the poisoned Kool-Aid. He came to church with me to see what I was getting into. My Bible study friends started praying unequally yoked prayers for me, and I prayed for Gordon's salvation. Pastor and everyone else told me to win him over quietly, but that was hard because I was on fire for God and telling everyone I met about Jesus. I am a naturally extroverted person anyway, and the church we were going to was Baptist. Bless their hearts they really did not know what to do with a Pentecostal like me. I remember when I was baptized in the swimming pool. Pastor Vosnos asked me to please not go swimming or start shouting or anything like that. Anyway, that August, during the *Book of Job* series of preaching, Gordon accepted Jesus into his heart, and all that worrying Gordon had done was for nothing because God had Gordon in his hand all along.

A lot has happened in the twenty-six years I have been serving Christ. The Navy brought us to California, then to Bremerton, and then to Port Orchard, Washington. We went from a Baptist church, to Nazarene, to Chico Alliance, to Pentecostal, and finally to The Christian Life Center. My kids grew up and moved away. I still struggle with food and codependent behaviors.

In 2003, weighing almost 300 pounds, I had gastric bypass surgery and got down to 160 pounds. Finally my church opened up a Celebrate Recovery Group. I learned about the Celebrate Recovery Program during Family Days, which is a big outreach our church has once a year. I did not go, though, until February 20, 2007. I don't know why I did not go earlier. The first time I went I felt at home. Then I went a couple more times to check it out. The third time I asked for a sponsor. That is how I got into recovery. Working the steps helped me get to know myself better, and that is a good thing. Working through my character defects was an eye opener, and it helped me understand myself. Working on the amends really touched me, because I got closure for hurts that were very old and deep. I thought I had closure on them long ago, but I did not. Amends are when you forgive people who have hurt you and you ask for forgiveness from people you have hurt whenever possible.

My relationship to others is more relaxed. I realize I can't fix them. I can't fix me, and I can't fix them—only God can. I accept them the way they are. Before, I would have tried to fix people to make their lives better for them. When I see myself doing that now, I take a deep breath and remember only God can fix someone, and then I try to relax and let go.

My relationship with God has changed. I worship more. I spend more time with Him. I am closer to Him. I pray more. I talk to Him like He is a regular Joe, because I was intimidated by Him before. The benefits of working the program are what I have mentioned before: closer relationships to God and others and more confidence in myself.

I would tell a newcomer to come and see the program and see that it works. By getting a sponsor and doing the steps and showing up for meetings, your life will change for the better. It worked for me.

TIM

I'm a believer who struggled with alcohol, drugs, sex, codependency, and food addictions. Before I found recovery, my life had become insane. I wasted a lot of years before I was willing to admit that. Actually my life seemed pretty normal to me. I said that everything seemed fine. As long as I wasn't hurting anyone, I didn't see a problem with what I was doing.

I grew up in a family that didn't know how to show love and affection. My parents were physically there but not emotionally available. Positive affirmations did not exist. About the only thing that we knew how to share were meals together. Looking back, my parents were struggling with their own addictions. We did some of the normal things that families do, so to the outside world it may have seemed that things were normal with us.

Inside our home there were many secrets. We never really communicated. Looking back over the childhood years, there were so many things out of control in our home that needed to be dealt with, but I didn't recognize that all the time. Cigarette smoking was the norm for all of us. By the time I was twelve, I was a full-blown smoker. My siblings were smokers as well. It was never mentioned that it was unhealthy for us or that we shouldn't steal the cigarettes from our parents.

From the time I was a young boy, pornography was readily available to me. I don't know if my parents knew that I was looking at it or not, but it wasn't hidden so I just assumed that it was fair game when I ran across it.

I have forgiven and do not blame my parents for feeding any of my addictions. Growing up I could have wished for more guidance, but in my later years I definitely made my own choices and somehow knew what was right from what was wrong.

By the time I hit my early teens, I was not only a smoker but had begun to dabble in drugs and alcohol as well. I was delivering newspapers with my friend and would go into homes when the owners were not there and steal the drugs from their medicine cabinets. I would take the drugs that I stole to school and sell them to others so that I could buy my drug of choice. I stole from grocery stores as well as from my friends and family to purchase drugs. I can remember going on outings with my family where all the adults would be drinking. After the adults were done with the alcohol, I would claim whatever was left to be mine. I don't know if they didn't notice, or just found it unimportant. Nothing was ever said about the missing alcohol.

We moved several times through out my childhood. I never felt very stable in any new environment. I always had so much fear of rejection that I never really took the chance to meet too many people. I had very few friends. I guess you could say that I was a loner. That is what I found the most comfortable. Looking back, the few friends that I did have practiced the same self-destructive behaviors that I did, and I can see now that I had found a comfort zone in those relationships. I never really felt like I could fit in anywhere else. Most of the time, I felt extremely lonely.

By the time I reached my high school years I had fallen heavily into drugs and alcohol. Loneliness and fear made these addictions a great companion. It didn't matter how I got the alcohol or drugs just as long as I got them. When I did make it to school, I felt awkward and different from everyone else. I eventually quit high school, as attending school no longer matched my lifestyle.

As drugs and alcohol began to take over my life, I began to experience blackouts. At times I would wake up in the morning with no recollection of the night before. I remember an incident of waking up in a hay field with a rock as my pillow.

When I started seeking employment, I sought out jobs that had little or no accountability to them. I didn't use alcohol when I was at work, but I did find a way to continue my drug use. As time went on I sank deeper and deeper into my shell. I never bothered moving out on my own. Without bills to pay I could earn just enough at work to keep up with my drug habits.

I continued living with all of my addictive behaviors. Sexual impurity became a part of my everyday thought life as well as in my everyday living. I eventually did move out on my own when I was twenty-six years old. I moved in with my girlfriend. My lifestyle however, did not change. Eventually she left, and I went into a deep depression. Being alone again, I sank even deeper into all of my addictions.

Not being able to financially make it on my own, I moved in with a roommate. I began to go to the bars with him. The bars became a great place to meet people and yet not let them know who I really was.

When I was twenty-eight, I met my wife. She was married, and we began to have an adulterous relationship. When we first met, we created a small world of our own, filled with drugs, alcohol, and lust. She went through a divorce, and we were married about a year and a half later. Things were very rocky between us. I had moved in with all of my addictions as well as my belongings. We had many suitcase drills. Although I loved her with all of my heart, I didn't know how to show her that love.

After I had known her for a few months, she made a decision that drugs and alcohol would not fit into her life any longer and that I needed to stop using if I was going to be a part of her life. She had three children and needed them to be her first priority and wanted me to consider them as well. This was hard for me. During my adult life, I had never really lived without being in some sort of an altered state. Reality without the use of drugs was so harsh.

My wife taught me about Jesus, and we had gone to church a few times. She taught me about prayer and said that God could help me with my addictions. Before that I had little to no knowledge of the Lord or His love for me. My wife had been involved in Twelve Step Programs for many years, and this information helped me so much. God did deliver me from drugs and alcohol. I didn't ask for help with the rest of my addictions. I didn't think that they were a problem.

After we were married, the behaviors that I had held at bay eventually came back. I was able to justify that it wasn't that bad because I wasn't using drugs or alcohol. The word "humble" was not in my dictionary. My drug of choice had now become pornography and an impure thought life.

When I was practicing my addictions, I believed that I wouldn't get caught. I was very cocky and very wrong. My wife did find out! She was devastated. She told me that I had to move out. Of course that affected our children as well. I understood why she would ask me to leave, but at the same time I was afraid that if I left she would never let me come back. I believe this was when I hit bottom. Through my unfaithfulness, my marriage was a wreck, and I had nowhere to look but up. I had been praying and going to church periodically, but I had not asked Jesus into my heart and turned my life over to Him.

I moved in with some friends of ours who had experienced their own trials with addictions. Their marriage had suffered because of their lifestyle, but they had begun the healing process. So, this was the right place for me to be. I spent many hours talking with my friends, reading scripture, and then praying for the rest of the night for my marriage, my family, and myself to be saved. God showed me through His word that night what needed to be changed in order for my marriage to be saved. I promised Him that I would work for Him for the rest of my life.

My recovery began with the realization of a need for a change in my life. I started attending church on a regular basis. I began counseling with a counselor who specialized in men with addictions. I found a group at church where I was able to share my experiences with other men that I could relate with, and I began to have hope. I learned that I needed to be accountable not only to myself but also with God and others.

By attending the group STAND, I learned that through each other we can gain strength to continue in our recovery, and by sharing with each other (giving it away) we could eventually begin to help others.

God did restore my marriage. My wife called one day, needing help to clear out the driveway. After I had that done, we lost power and I ended up being snowed in. God had given us the time together to begin to talk, sort out our lives, and start healing. It was just the very beginning.

I would like to say that things were perfect from then on, but it would be the furthest thing from the truth. Things were very unstable for quite a long time. I did revert back to some of my addictions and came to realize that I had to look much deeper inside of myself. This time I had God to turn to instead of my addictions.

A couple of years later I awoke from a dream in the middle of the night. It felt like my soul was broken. I had never had such a deep ache in my heart. The dream was so vivid it felt like I was experiencing a death. I realized that the sin that I was dealing with in my life had been passed on to me from the generations before me.

In the dream I felt that God was showing me that I had to choose not to pass these addictions on to my children. And how the Father dances over our victories and cries over our sin. I realized that He had been watching me over the years and how it had broken His heart that His child was so in need yet had not asked for his needs to be met.

Through working the Fourth and Fifth Steps, I learned how to confess my faults and remain humble. "If we confess our sins, He is faithful and just to forgive us our sins and to cleanse us from all unrighteousness" (1 John 1:9, NKJV). Step Ten has shown me that I need to keep a daily inventory (looking in the mirror).

Through the restoration of my marriage and family, and working the steps of the program, God has taught me not to judge others. "Do to others, as you would have them do to you" (Luke 6:31, NIV). "Do not judge, or you too will be judged. For in the same way you judge others, you will be judged, and with the measure you use, it will be measured to you" (Matthew 7:1-2, NIV). "So, if you think you are standing firm, be careful that you don't fall!" (1 Cor 10:12, NIV).

I have come to realize through my relationship with God, my wife and children, church family and friends that life is not about me, but what I can pour into others. "I have told you these things, so that in me you may have peace. In this world you will have trouble. But take heart! I have overcome the world" (John 16:33, NIV). This verse has come to mean so much to me as my life has had many trials.

In four years, I have lost my mother, father, and both brothers, not to mention the loss of both grandparents. In 2005, our twenty-five-year-old daughter passed away in her sleep due to a problem with her heart that we were not aware of. Her five-year-old daughter was the one who found her in the morning. Life has been difficult and has had many abrupt changes since that day. I was beginning to relate quite well to a famous man in the Bible by the name of Job. In the past, I never would have made it through these experiences without finding comfort in at least one of my addictions. However, God brought me through, not without pain or fear, but through

His grace and mercy I have been able to maintain my recovery through Celebrate Recovery. My favorite song says something like, "Where there is faith, there is a voice calling, 'Keep walking; you're not alone in this world.'" How true that has been for me, and it can be true for you as well.

SUGGESTED READING

Alcoholics Anonymous. *Dr. Bob and the Good Oldtimers.* New York City, NY: A.A. World Services, 1980.

B., Mel. *New Wine:* Hazelden Foundation, 1991.

Barnett, Tommy. *There's A Miracle in Your House.* Lake Mary, FL: Charisma House, 1993.

Beattie, Melody. *Codependents' Guide to the Twelve Steps.* New York, NY: Prentice Hall Press, 1990.

Bosworth, F.F. *Christ The Healer.* New Kensington, PA: Whitaker House, 2000.

Bounds, E.M. *The Complete Works of E.M. Bounds:* Baker Books, 1990.

Bynum, Juanita. *Praying From The Third Dimension.* Queens, NY: Holman Bible Publishers, 1998.

Bynum, Juanita. *The Threshing Floor.* Lake Mary, FL: Charisma House, 2005.

Christenson, Evelyn. *A Time to Pray God's Way.* Eugene, OR: Harvest House Publishers, 1996.

Copeland, Germaine. *Prayers That Avail Much.* Tulsa, OK: Harrison House, 1997.

Cornwall, Judson. *Praying the Scriptures.* Lake May, FL: Creation House, 1988.

Doe, Father John. *Sobriety and Beyond.* Center City, MN: Hazelden, 1955.

Doe, Father John. *Sobriety Without End.* Center City, MN: Hazelden, 1957.

Donahue, Anita Corrine. *When I'm on My Knees:* Uhrichsville, OH: Barbour Books.

Dunn, Ronald. *Don't Just Stand There, Pray Something.* Nashville, TN: Thomas Nelson Inc., 1992.

Goll, Jim W. *Intercession.* Sheppensberg, PA: Destiny Image Publishers, 2003.

Goll, Jim W. *The Lost Art of Intercession.* Sheppensberg, PA: Destiny Image Publishers, 1997.

Goll, Jim W. *Kneeling on the Promises.* Grand Rapids, MI: Chosen Books, 1999.

Hess, Tom. *The Watchmen.* Washington, DC: Progressive Vision International, 1998.

Hinn, Benny. *Prayers That Get Results.* Dallas TX: Clarion Call Marketing, 2005.

Huch, Larry. *Free At Last.* Portland, OR: Larry Huch Ministries, 2000.

Lake, John G. *Spiritual Hunger and other Sermons.* Dallas, TX: Christ For The Nations, Inc., 1987.

Munroe, Myles Dr. *Prayer.* New Kensington, PA: Whitaker House, 2002.

Murray, Andrew. *With Christ in the School Of Prayer.* Whitaker House, 1981.

Murray, Andrew. *The Secret of Intercession.* New Kensington, PA: Whitaker House, 1995.

Omatian, Stormie. *The Power of a Praying Woman.* Eugene, OR: Harvest House Pub, 2002.

Pierce, Chuck D. *Prayers That Outwit the Enemy.* Ventura, CA: Regal Books, 2004.

Sheets, Dutch. *Intercessory Prayer,* Ventura, CA: Regal Books, 1996.

Tenney, Tommy. *Prayers of a God Chaser.* Bloomington, MN: Bethany House Publishers, 1987.

Van Arsdall, LaNora. *40 Days to Freedom*. Gilbert, AZ: Fountain Gate Ministries, 2006.

Wagner, C. Peter. *Prayer Shield*. Ventura, CA: Regal Books, 1992.

Wilkerson, Bruce. *The Prayer of Jabez*: Multnomah Publisher, 2000.

Yoder, Barbara J. *The Breaker Anointing*. Ventura, CA: Regal Books, 2002.

Selected Bibliography

Alcoholics Anonymous. *A.A. Big Book 3ʳᵈ Ed.* New York City, NY: A.A. World Services, 1976.

Alcoholics Anonymous. *Twelve Steps and Twelve Traditions.* New York City, NY: A.A. World Services 1981.

B., Dick. *A.A. Roots in the Bible.* www.dickb.com.

Bright, Bill. *Have You Heard of the Four Spiritual Laws?* San Bernardino, CA: Campus Crusade, 1965.

Cash, Johnny, *The Gospel Road Documentary.* The Luther Corp., 1972.

Cash, Johnny. *The Man in White.* San Francisco, CA: Harper & Row, 1986.

Cook, Jerry. *Love, Acceptance & Forgiveness.* Ventura, CA: Regal Books, 1979.

Ford, John C. Depth Psychology and Compulsion-Alcoholism and Moral Responsibility, Weston, MA: Weston College Press, 1951.

Fox, Emmet. *The Sermon on the Mount.* New York, NY: Harper & Row, Publishers, 1938.

Graham, Billy. *How To Be Born Again.* Waco, TX: Word Books Publisher, 1977.

Graham, Franklin. *The Name.* Nashville, TN: Thomas Nelson, Inc., 2002.

Hill, Stephen. *A Time To Weep.* Lake Mary, FL: Creation House, 1997.

May, Gerald G. *Addiction & Grace.* San Francisco, CA: Harper Collins Publishers, 1988.

Oursler, Will. *The Healing Power of Faith.* New York, NY: Berkley Books, 1991.

Peck, M. Scott. *The Road Less Traveled.* New York, NY: Simon & Schuster, 1998.

Peck, M. Scott. *The People of the Lie.* New York, NY: Simon & Schuster, 1983.

Tenney, Tommy. *Chasing God, Serving Man.* Shippensburg, PA. Destiny Image Publishers, 2001.

Warren, Rick. *The Purpose-Driven Life.* Grand Rapids, MI: Zondervan, 2002.